BROTHER-SPIRIT

Also by Tom Owen-Towle:

BROTHER-SPIRIT

MEN JOINING TOGETHER IN THE QUEST FOR INTIMACY AND ULTIMACY

BY

Tom Owen-Towle

Bald Eagle Mountain Press
P. O. Box 4314
San Diego, California 92164

The pages of this edition are printed on recycled paper.

FIRST EDITION.

ISBN 0-9630636-0-X

DEDICATIONS

With profound acknowledgment and appreciation, I dedicate this book to the following companions:

— To my brother-in-law, Tony Sheets, whose painting graces the cover and who, upon hearing four years ago that I was considering this project, told me: "Tom, this is a necessary book. Pursue it!"

— To my soul-brother, Chris Hassett, who has labored to make this text ready for publication and, moreover, has given me critical encouragement all along the way.

— To my life-partner, Carolyn, an ardent feminist *and* unswerving supporter of my Brother-Spirit quest. We walk our sacred paths alone . . . together.

— To all my brothers, known and unknown, points West and East, North and South, who pursue intimacy and ultimacy in their daily lives.

Foreword

The second great wave of the women's movement has been with us for the past quarter century, and feminist women have been vigorously exploring their own lives as full human beings moving toward liberation from oppression. Belatedly — but surely — men have begun to do likewise. The men's movement has come more slowly and haltingly, and that is understandable. Those who are in power, those who have considered themselves humanly normative generally have much less motivation to question their own lives. But the men's movement is now well under way. One of the clues to that is the expanding number of books being written on men's issues. To date, however, few writers have ventured beyond the psychological or sociological focus into the realm of the spiritual. Tom Owen-Towle is one of the few exceptions, and it is a distinct honor to introduce his second volume.

Like his first, this second book from his pen shows a remarkable sensitivity to men's religious quests. The author does not assume that all men are on the same spiritual journey. Those journeys take many different forms, given the idiosyncrasies of our particular histories, not to mention our different life situations shaped by age, race, social class, and sexual orientation. Nevertheless, with St. Augustine, Tom Owen-Towle knows well the fact that describes us all: "Thou hast created us for thyself, O God, and our hearts are restless until they find their rest in thee."

That restlessness — a *creative* restlessness — is probed richly in these pages. The author looks freshly at a number of male relationships depicted in the Bible, and in doing so he makes familiar stories leap from the page with new insights about men's wounds and men's healing. As if he were holding up a diamond into the sun and slowly turning it to catch varied refractions of light, he holds up men's religious pilgrimages and illumines them facet by facet. He takes us into the male-bonding circles to show us the problems and the enormous possibilities of men's ritual and support groups. He elucidates the common themes of the Brother-Spirit journey, themes which benefit the reader in private meditation as well as providing an exciting agenda for men's groups. In all of this there is the tone of balance: balance between the inner and the outer, the spiritual and the worldly.

I would like, particularly, to comment on four important dimensions of these pages. I find each of them important in its own right as a hopeful path for men on the Brother-Spirit journey, and together they make this book rich, indeed.

The first is *personal story*. We men (particularly we white Western men) have long been accomplished in objective, rational discourse. Such discourse serves important purposes. It does not, however, suffice to reach the soul depths or to probe the deep masculinity that we so want and need. For that the vulnerability of personal story is necessary. The author knows that well, and these pages are richly laced with significant pieces of his own life.

Intimacy and ultimacy are the second dimension. Tom Owen-Towle identifies these hungers at the outset, and the themes permeate the book. I find them significant in the interrelation, as does he. It is common knowledge that countless men are hungering for more relational intimacy these days. And from time immemorial men have hungered for ultimacy — for engaging the divine. What the author sees clearly and powerfully is that each needs the other. Authentic intimacy with others drives us to depths of spirit, and unless we are open to the latter our experiences of intimacy remain too shallow. And, we deceive ourselves (as male theologians frequently have done) if we think that engagement with God can take place with any profundity apart from our intimacy with others.

This brings me to the third dimension, which I shall call the *incarnational* one. So much of Christian theology has confined incarnation — the embodiment of God in human flesh — to one figure, Jesus of Nazareth. In doing so, such theology has perpetuated the spirit-body dualism that has been such a crippling problem for so many centuries. The logic seems to go like this: since spirit is really antithetical to body, and since God is truly spirit, the embodiment of God can happen only by special miracle, and that has happened only once, for our salvation. Tom Owen-Towle knows well that this kind of dualism truncates the depth meanings of both spirit and body. He knows well that incarnation is a possibility and, in some sense at least, a reality for all of us — and that is our hope. Men particularly need to hear this good news.

Finally, I want to comment on the author's *feminism.* Throughout the book two different-but-related claims are clear: one, feminism and the agenda of gender justice and reconciliation must be a top priority and urgent mission for men; two, there is a distinctive male agenda which is not the same as women's agenda. I find both of these — and both of them held together — utterly important. It is easy to fall into one to the neglect of the other, and there are ample evidences of this in the men's movement and its literature. It is much more difficult to hold them together, but we must. Justice, the healing of a fragile and wounded planet, and our male fulfillment all depend on both together. This, too, Tom Owen-Towle knows well.

Surely there are other strengths of this book. The wealth of evocative quotations is one. The practical helpfulness of the author's experience for guiding men's groups and gatherings is another. His breadth of reading in the relevant literature and his bibliographies are still another. But enough! It is time for the reader to begin a rewarding immersion in these pages, which I am delighted to introduce.

James B. Nelson
Professor of Christian Ethics
United Theological Seminary of the Twin Cities

TABLE OF CONTENTS

INTRODUCTION

Be a Columbus to whole new continents and worlds within
you, opening new channels not of trade, but of thought. [1]
— Henry David Thoreau

I was a shy, inward child. My parents relate that I didn't talk
much until I was five years old. During this withdrawn period I had
ample opportunity to cultivate my private life, to swim amid the
depths, to dream, to dance with inner mysteries.

Then, as a teenager, I was impressed when Jesus' mother Mary
(my mother's name too) took the world's wonders and woes and
"pondered them in her heart." That sounded like a worthy vocation
to follow, not just for women, or mothers, but for us men too.

In my early twenties I entered the ministry to feed my yearnings
for further reflection and soulful retreat.

At mid-stream in my career, at the age of forty-four, I took a
sabbatical. I had served, struggled, and produced without a significant break for two decades. I now had five months to study, write,
travel, be with family, and most of all, to take stock. After all, Sabbath
means to desist from frantic ways, to "catch one's breath."

My sabbatical pilgrimage came in the nick of time. I had no idea
how out of spiritual steam I was. I had been caught up in the typical
ministerial frenzy of activism and ambition, and I was burning low.
My soul's gauge read "nearly empty."

I realized, to my chagrin, that the bulk of my ministry had been
"doing" — planning, talking, healing, expending my time, energy,
and talents. Little of my vocation had been spent in reflection. I had
all but forsaken my early proclivity and passion for silence. Like so
many of my colleagues I had effectively sidestepped my vow to ponder
things in my heart.

In the first week of my sabbatical, I was sick as a dog — fever-
ish, trembling, achy all over, exhausted.

After two weeks of falling apart, my wife Carolyn and I were fortuitously scheduled to attend a Spiritual Discipline retreat at my old seminary in the Bay Area. I knew I needed intellectual stimulation, solitude, and time with my beloved, but I was unprepared for my appetite for the spiritual fare of the conference: chanting, serene walks, prayer, silence, spiritual story exchanges.

I came starved. I left replete. It was a transformative week for me spiritually and as a male. My Brother-Spirit quest was taking shape. I started to brew this book.

Brother-Spirit is about the inseparable quests of adult men for intimacy as brothers and ultimacy as spiritual travelers. It is the story of me and Howard, Dick, Paul, Nathan, Chris, Joe, Michael, George, Ed, Bob, Kurt, John, David, Rick, Bob, Doug, Everardo and innumerable other men in my circle and beyond who find it imperative to shape spiritual life together for the remainder of our days.

Men have done amazing things throughout history. Some glorious, some awful. We have wrestled in sports. We have built bridges of all kinds. We have locked horns and clinched deals in the business world. We have fought alongside and against one another in war.

Of late, men have searched for excellence, prosperity, our identities. But our most important, arduous expedition lies largely unexplored. It is the sacred quest through inner landscape, the journey to fulfill our deep, persistent yearnings for intimacy or fellowship and ultimacy or meaning.

By intimacy I refer to warm, close bonds grown through sharing our minds and hearts. By birth we are inescapably men; by choice we become brothers to other men, women, animals, divinity.

Intimacy denotes sexual familiarity in today's parlance, but this need not be the case. Intimacy comes from *intimata,* which refers to the innermost coats of our organs. They are the layers backed by connective and elastic tissue. Therefore, when men are intimate with one another, we are open to the innermost connective and elastic tissues of our selves. In Old Testament language, we reveal our interiors, "calling deep unto deep." This process of intimacy among men is brothering.

By ultimacy this book is concerned with those values and aspirations which are fundamental, utmost, crowning, carriers of fulfillment for men. Although my understanding of ultimacy includes matters of divine mystery and disclosure, it should be noted that dictionary definitions of "ultimacy" do not refer explicitly to deity.

It is the contention of Brother-Spirit that intimacy and ultimacy are intertwining and mutually reinforcing quests. Men suffer from twin hungers: we hunger both for friendship and meaning, companionship and completion, warmth and depth, community and purpose in our lives. Men become truly intimate with our brothers and others, as we wrestle together with the ultimate issues of existence.

This volume, as with my earlier one, *New Men — Deeper Hungers,* is aimed primarily at men. Why? First, because I am a middle-aged, male minister and can only accurately speak of my own gender's quest for meaning.

Second, women are far ahead of men in matters of the spirit. The field of feminist theology is flourishing. Little has been composed by men, for men, in the area of spiritual companionship and discipline.

Third, men reside in a quandary. We can't return to the stifling, demeaning, sexist ways of patriarchal religion where everything has been male-dominated.

Patriarchal religion has been oppressive to women and undermining of authentic maleness. Men like myself are interested neither in subjugating ourselves to a Father-God nor in dominating women or earth.

However, we can't merely react to or build upon feminist theology either. It doesn't speak of our direct experience. Our male identity will remain uncertain until we establish a fresh version of spirituality which grows out of the soil of male pride, wounds, affection, and hope. Brother-Spirit is such an effort. It is a spirituality spun alongside not over-against feminist spirituality. It pursues peace-making with self, women, men, children, earth, and divinity.

There are five sections in *Brother-Spirit:* "Origins," "Journey," "Circles," "Themes," and "Balance."

"Origins" centers upon pivotal male relationships in the Bible: fathers and sons, brothers, and a family of men. Traditionally, the Bible has been read through patriarchal eyes, lately the feminist lens. I invite readers to lift up biblical stories and motifs and view them from the theological perspective of Brother-Spirit. I have selected male-male exchanges in both the Old and New Testaments to illustrate various dimensions of Brother-Spirit.

There are also ample, useful brothering encounters in Eastern religious literature, such as the Gilgamesh Epic, or in Greek mythology, but I have chosen to emphasize Western scriptures because they are most familiar to American men. Indeed, the path of our lives has been inescapably shaped by such Old Testament male-male confrontations as Father-God and Adam, Cain and Abel, Abraham and Isaac, David and Absalom, Esau and Jacob, Joseph and his brothers, Moses and Aaron, and David and Jonathan *and* the range of emotions they embodied — hostility, affection, deceit, teamwork, jealousy, and reconciliation. It is my belief that these primal biblical encounters between men need revisioning.

In the New Testament I have focused on the Prodigal Son story where father-son issues as well as brother-brother dynamics are explored, and upon Jesus, as our elder brother rather than prophet or savior.

The second portion of *Brother-Spirit,* entitled "Journey," centers on the spiritual quest of men: describing the elements, dangers, and benefits of the religious pilgrimage. This section highlights the similarities and differences between Brother-Spirit and the traditional monastic movement as well as contemporary feminist religious thought.

After depicting what it might mean for modern men to become brothers of Jacob (Old Testament) and brothers of Joseph (New Testament), men who will be equally brothers and feminists, we move to the third section of *Brother-Spirit,* called "Circles," which explores the need of men to band together in male-identified support and search groups. The challenges of men-only groups are also noted.

Four fundamental attitudes are required for Brother-Spirit circles. First, men are encouraged to speak confessionally rather than rationally and dispassionately. Second, we are asked to work collegially rather than self-sufficiently in our Brother-Spirit venture. Third, we are invited to broaden our religious expressiveness with non-verbal experiences such as song, ritual, and play. Finally, men are called to become questioners instead of our conventional role as answer-givers.

The Brother-Spirit course which I have developed engages thirteen religious "Themes." These are evocative, not exhaustive, motifs for intimates to explicate on the ultimacy quest:

1) Re-Membering Our Past

2) Fulfilling Our Selves

3) Loving Our Neighbors

4) Pursuing Truths

5) Engaging Our Brothers

6) Making Peace With the Earth

7) Honoring Our God

8) Becoming Good Fathers and Good Sons

9) Meshing Sexuality and Spirituality

10) Exploring Deep Wisdom

11) Welcoming Wonder

12) Healing Our Wounds

13) Facing Death and Beyond

The closing section, entitled "Balance," urges men to move from the mountains of spiritual refreshment and challenge back to the valleys of daily life, sharing the wisdom and maturity gained in retreat with our work situations and family relationships. This has been the rhythm of holy activists throughout human history. Maintaining one's balance, inner and outer, is the final hope of our Brother-Spirit journey.

Brother-Spirit is a movement whose time has come for men. As religious forebrother, A. Powell Davies, remarked: "All life is a chance to grow a soul." Now is the call and opportunity for men to risk growing our souls in companionship with one another.

Brother-Spirit heralds a new age with its revolutionary process and nourishing course of action for men and the women who choose to share in their growing.

ORIGINS

FATHERS AND SONS

Speaking of sacred texts, Heinrich Zimmer wrote:

> They are everlasting oracles of life. They have to be
> questioned and consulted anew, with every age, each age
> approaching them with its own variety of ignorance and
> understanding, its own set of problems and its own
> inevitable questions.[1]
>
> — *The King and the Corpse*

There are women and men alike who contend that the Bible as
a sacred text is irredeemably patriarchal, therefore useless. Yet contemporary feminist theologians like Rosemary Radford Ruether and
Elizabeth Schüssler Fiorenza have stayed within the Judeo-Christian
fold and reinterpreted the biblical materials to combat patriarchy and
create justice and compassion for all people.

It is time for sensitive, searching men to revisit the familiar stories of the Bible with an eye not for dogma or defense but for what
they might contribute to our being more mature sons, fathers,
brothers, friends, and partners.

Male theologians have traditionally read the Bible to construct
theories of sin and salvation, grow sermons, and develop scholarly
tomes and systematic theologies. The biblical drama can also yield

psycho-spiritual insights for our male lives.

The Bible, filled with realistic stories and relevant parables, is a treasure trove of wisdom for contemporary men who hunger to be more confessional, intimate, responsible people alongside other men, women, the natural world, and God.

There is a growing number of American men who are more concerned with satisfying relationships than tight doctrines. Being a male-dominant volume, the Bible presents an overwhelming array of men to study. For the purposes of my Brother-Spirit approach, I have chosen to analyze men in relationship, because men are least developed as social beings, especially in friendship with other men.

Since intimacy or brothering is a primary theme of Brother-Spirit, I will be observing what Old Testament encounters like God–Adam, Cain–Abel, Abraham–Isaac, David–Absalom, Esau–Jacob, Joseph–brothers, Moses–Aaron, and Jonathan–David have to teach us as new men. One could also focus profitably upon Jonah, Job, and other biblical portraits of men in relationship.

In the New Testament, I look at the Prodigal Son story with its multiple male-male exchanges and at Jesus as a brother figure for modern men rather than the traditional prophet, savior, and Lord.

It has been the custom of male theologians to treat the men in the Bible essentially as either larger or lower than life: as gods, heroes, giants, and patriarchs or as killers, servants, and scoundrels. Men move toward greater intimacy and ultimacy in our lives when we look *across* at our fellow men rather than look *up* or *down* at them.

We covet peers who are more like us than not, who know our fears, angers, affections, alienations, and yearnings. Such men and their stories exist in Old and New Testament episodes. Whereas the Bible can be debated heatedly as a theological treatise, it is quite lucid and cogent in its depiction of flesh-and-blood men and women.

The biblical portraits of men in relationship are particularly relevant to our Brother-Spirit quest because they are so true to life. We men recognize ourselves when Cain kills Abel, when Jacob and Esau are reconciled, when Moses and Aaron work as teammates, and when Jonathan and David declare their unswerving, mutual affection. We acknowledge our own flaws, our ambivalences, our capabilities upon visiting our male forebears in the pages of the Bible.

The Wound That Renews Itself

My thesis is that the father-son dynamic and resolution influences greatly all male-male interactions which follow. This is true in biblical lore and our contemporary lives, whether we are speaking theologically or biologically, about our "heavenly" or "earthly" fathers. As with the case of God–Adam, then Cain–Abel, so also with their descendants. The blockage we men experience in our relationships with our fathers is worked out, usually in unsatisfactory and often damaging fashion with our brothers. To put it another way, because we are unresolved in our vertical, authority relationships, our horizontal, peer encounters suffer a consequential price.

Perry Garfinkel validates this claim in his own study of "Fathers and Sons: After His Image":

> The father is not all he appears at first to be. In fact,
> as most of the men in my research indicate, the men
> they wanted to love the most and be closest to — their
> fathers — were the ones with whom they were least able
> to feel intimate. The ally is revealed as the rival. . . . The
> father-son relationship is a microcosm and a model of
> how men relate to each other.[2]

Thus our primary hurt, gap, wound is with our fathers, which then gets replayed, often exacerbated, in the wounding of our peers. In sum, hurt men inevitably hurt others.

Since I am moving metaphorically back and forth between theological and biological relationships, it is worthwhile to discern how the encounter between Father-God and Adam unfolds and colors Adam's relationship to his sons, Cain and Abel. Adam is essentially an absentee father with respect to his sons. He has sexual intercourse twice in verses 1 and 2, then disappears for the remainder of the chapter and his sons' lives. He plays a minimal role according to Genesis 4 and is noticeably unavailable when his sons get into life-and-death trouble. An all-too-familiar portrait of twentieth-century American fathers.

Andrew Melton describes the "father hunger" in this way:

> The main business of the father's life was not here with
> the family, but somewhere else, somewhere outside,
> where life was played out in a broader sphere, which in
> his son's imagination was much more fascinating, much

more exciting. But intimacy is not something that can be learned from an abstraction.[3]

Melton goes on:

> And this is why father hunger tends to be passed from generation to generation — why the son of a father-hungry father will be father-hungry himself.[4]

Sam Osherson, in his pioneering work called *Finding Our Fathers: The Unfinished Business of Manhood,* says the same thing in a different way:

> Boys grow into men with a wounded father within; a conflicted inner sense of masculinity rooted in men's experience of their fathers as rejecting, incompetent, or absent.[5]

To rub salt into our already raw wounds, Elizabeth Dodson Gray, an ardent religious feminist, rightly observes:

> The classic defense of male-gender language about God, epitomized in the phrase "God the Father," is that God loves us as a father does. This is surely a strange patriarchal reversal, since we all know that most of the care in childhood did not come from our fathers. Rather, in sickness and in health, our nurturing almost invariably came from our mothers and from other women. Dorothy Boroush, a Unitarian Universalist minister, says she is going to produce another communion service, one which celebrates the nourishment we have all received from the body and blood of our mothers, blood poured out over the years for us.[6]

The father-son relationship is often marked by absenteeism, alienation, even abuse. We sons suffer profound father hunger and hurt. The mission of our lives is to fill that hunger and heal that hurt.

Adam learned well from his theological father. There are multiple motifs and exchanges among God, Adam, Eve, and the serpent worth study in the first three chapters of Genesis, but it can be stated fairly that God and Adam, father and son, have a fleeting, shallow tie. The first exchange with his son, Adam, resides in the form of a question: "Why are you hiding?" A question of ethics, not location. Whether following misbehavior or not, for the son, Adam, to be naked before his father, physically and emotionally, is awkward, even a source of embarrassment.

Adam tries to justify his wrongdoing by scapegoating his partner. The son ends up getting punished by his father via sweat and toil, the curse of death, and banishment from the garden.

In any case, the relationship between Father-God and Son-Adam is tenuous, somewhat tormented, hardly caring or intimate. Adam had a remote father, and he became one. He hid from God, then he hid from his sons.

I visualize Michelangelo's poignant, powerful depiction of God and Adam reaching out to touch one another on the ceiling of the Sistine Chapel. They grope, they extend, they stretch, but they do not touch. They do not connect. An unfulfilled relationship.

Judith Viorst, in her splendid work *Necessary Losses,* portrays the valiant yet "imperfect connection" between father and son as she recalls a passage from Herbert Gold's memoir-novel *Fathers,* where the hero, now middle-aged, takes his daughter to a skating rink, just as his father had taken him years ago:

> "I remember why skating with my father gave me such joy," he writes. "It was the hope of intimacy, waiting to be redeemed. . . . I believed the abyss between my father and me, between others and me, could be crossed. . . . Like a gangster I sought to penetrate my father's secret soul. The limits remained unredeemed." [7]

Plagued by partial, wounded, imperfect bonds, we fathers and sons struggle toward resolution all our days on earth. We valiantly try to break the cycle of hurt and hunger.

Fathers Play Favorites

Brothering starts inauspiciously with the envious Cain snuffing out the life of his kin Abel. This deadly blow provides the tragic paradigm for following generations. Men have been homicidal killers since the beginnings of biblical time.

Perry Garfinkel states:

> It's no secret that men have had trouble relating to each other ever since Cain killed Abel. The first-born son of Adam slew his younger brother when God chose Abel's

offering over his own. Thus was envy born; followed
quickly by violence.[8]

As blood brothers men are incorrigibly ambivalent. We feel both
closeness and jealousy. We are buddies; we are rivals. Sometimes we
break through to the other side as adults: confident and caring
brothers. Other times we go to our respective graves nursing sibling
grudges.

The competition sparked among brothers is writ large among
men in general. There is deceit, cruelty, even fratricide in our male
milieu today.

What happened? The story is scant: Cain, the first born is a tiller
of ground; Abel is a keeper of sheep. There is nothing unusual here,
for we brothers are often engaged in different ventures. It is also no
surprise that each brother brings special offerings from his respective
labor.

The first shock follows: God accepts Abel's gift and rejects Cain's.
This divine move is bewildering. Cain is dejected and angry. He then
lures Abel out into the fields, whereupon he attacks and kills his
brother. Thus begins our male inability to be angry without turning
hostile, to be filled with righteous rage without displaying destructive behavior.

Men have been slow to learn the charity of anger and quick to
convert our frustrations into violence.

But what is usually ignored or minimized in this story is God's
role. Father-God shows capricious behavior in favoring one son over
the other. There is no reason given for God's arbitrariness. What valid
explanation could be given?

Men recognize this scenario. Our fathers prefer the presence or
presents of one of us. Mothers show favoritism too (as we shall discover later on with Rebekah).

One brief aside. My brother Phil and I (three years apart) received minimal preferential treatment growing up. Yet recently in
recalling our shared childhood, we chuckled nervously when Phil
claimed that he felt he was the favored son and I thought I was.

Where were Adam and Eve during all this turmoil? Absentee
parents? Listen to the way Elie Wiesel extrapolates:

> Adam could not be found. He had disappeared. Van-
> ished. At the very moment when his presence was most

needed. While Cain was in trouble with God and Abel
was pitted against Cain, Adam was conspicuously absent.
As though the education and problems of his sons were
no concern of his. He was the busy father, overworked
and self-involved, earning his bread by the sweat of his
brow.[9]

What results from this favoritism? The brothers take it out on
one another. Hurt within, Cain lashes out. His envy translates into
violence. Instead of getting angry at God (at Dad), Cain slays his
innocent brother. Daniel Berrigan in recalling his painful relationship with his own father writes about the battle with his six brothers:

In those years our fighting and wrestling and internecine
rages were beyond limit in frequency and intensity.
Oppressed as we were, we worked out on one another the
pain of life with father.[10]

Oliver Stone's movie on Viet Nam, *Platoon,* raises some painful
truths, as noted by *Time* magazine:

American soldiers — the young men we sent there to do
our righteous dirty work — turned their frustrations
toward fratricide. In Viet Nam, G.I.s re-created the world
back home, with its antagonisms of race, region and class.
Finding no clear and honorable path to victory in the
booby-trapped underbrush, some grunts focused their
gunsights on their comrades. The Viet Cong and North
Vietnamese army were shadowy figures in this family
tragedy: stage center, it was sibling riflery. . . . Stone's
film asks of our soldiers, "Am I my brother's killer?" The
answer is an anguished yes.[11]

Elie Wiesel recounts the first genocide:

Did Cain suffer? Had God treated him unfairly? He
should have told God so. Had not God asked him the
question: "Why is your face so somber?" Cain could
have, should have answered. And said what was on his
mind. But he chose to remain silent, to swallow his
grudge and transform it into poisonous hate. In so doing,
he deprived himself of the right to judge God by killing
his brother.[12]

If only Cain had vented rather than violated. He had no right to
take anyone's life, especially his kin, but then we never do. Why didn't

the Berrigan boys tell their father off sometimes instead of pounding one another? Why didn't American sons resist their fatherland, or thumb their noses at Uncle Sam, instead of committing fratricide? Well, some did. But it's never easy to yell at Father-God, even when that is our right, our obligation, our hope.

Cain's problem is our male problem, the base pivotal psychological-social-spiritual malaise of our lives. We are livid with our Dad, with whom we share our initial male-dyad, and we can't release on our fury. We are thwarted; consequently, we inflict wounds on ourselves or our neighbors.

Dad is bigger, stronger, more articulate, in charge. We can't buck him. We are unable to criticize or confront him. There are other depictions in literature of the towering, hurtful father. One powerful piece comes from Nikos Kazantzakis in his autobiography, *Report to Greco:*

> I had never faced my father with a feeling of tenderness.
> The fear he called forth in me was so great that all the
> rest — love, respect, intimacy — vanished. His words
> were severe, his silence even more severe. He seldom
> spoke, and when he did open his mouth, his words were
> measured and well weighed; you could never find
> grounds to contradict him. He was always right, which
> seemed to make him invulnerable. . . . An oak he was,
> with a hard trunk, rough leaves, bitter fruit, and no
> flowers. He ate up all the strength around him; in his
> shade every other tree withered. I withered in his shade
> similarly. I did not want to live beneath his breath. . . .
> This is why I was forced to write down all I wished I had
> done, instead of becoming a great struggler in the realm
> of action — from fear of my father. He it was who
> reduced my blood to ink. . . . I had feared only one man
> in my life: my father. . . . He alone remained always as I
> had seen him in my childhood: a giant. Towering in
> front of me, he blocked my share of the sun.[13]

We seldom are able to confront this giant who blocks our share of the sun. Yet the earlier and more frequently we display appropriate anger at Father-God as a son, the healthier our adult male-male bonds will be. Our troubles in relating adequately to other men largely stem from unresolved frustrations and unexpressed anger toward our fathers — both earthly and heavenly.

But Cain and Abel were adults, not children, weren't they? Yes. It just shows that as adult males we still haven't dealt constructively with our hurt feelings as sons. Cain was an adult *and* deferred to a capricious father.

Father-God banishes son-Cain from his land, his profession, his dignity, and his Dad's presence. Cain is destined to tramp across the earth forever, shifting from farmer to fugitive.

Men have lived with this curse throughout the centuries, wandering, often aimlessly, from place to place, person to person, fascination to fascination. We have been out of sync with ourselves, earth, others, family, divinity.

We have seldom known intimacy or ultimacy, the very quests for which we were born. Brother-Spirit is a religious course to restore men's imbalance, to bring Cains back to our homes: ourselves, our kin, our Father-God.

Cain is distraught. He must relinquish everything important to him and he stands to lose his very life. He cries out, no longer in arrogance or defiance, but in fright and anguish. "My punishment is greater than I can bear." Cain, who in killing, defended and dehumanized himself, now regains some sense of humanity. Hitting bottom, Cain is open to being helped.

Father-God has a change of heart as well. He who began capriciously, ends this encounter with his offspring, compassionately. God shows mercy. He puts an identifying mark on his son to ward off attackers.

God and Cain, father and son, part forever. Twentieth-century American men are the spiritual heirs of this primal encounter.

Sacrificial Sons

> What is it with these fathers who want to destroy their
> children? . . . Whence comes this royal and noble
> willingness to spill the blood of their offspring? Saul and
> Jonathan, Saturn and Chronus, then Chronus and Zeus.
> Abraham and Isaac, Laius and Oedipus, Agamemnon and
> Iphigenia, Jephthah and his daughter — the list is long. I
> never hated Absalom. I know if I were God and possessed
> His powers, I would sooner obliterate the world I had
> created than allow any child of mine to be killed in it, for

any reason whatsoever. I would have given my own life to save my baby's, and even to spare Absalom's. But that may be because I am Jewish, and God is not.[14]

— Joseph Heller, *God Knows*

There are other Old Testament illustrations of the primary father-son wound or unfulfilled bond. Each example leads to a worsening of the father-son connection in ensuing generations. Alas, the biblical prophecy is fulfilled: "and the sins of the fathers are visited upon the sons."

Andrew Schmookler notes our transgenerational abusiveness in his book, *Out of Weakness: Healing the Wounds That Drive Us to War:*

> It is obvious that the wielders of power are, with few exceptions, men. . . . Pathologies of the will afflict not only those on the bottom, but also — and in some cases especially — those who ride them on top. Even the dominant do not begin on top. Even members of the ruling class begin as children, often subject to a socialization process of systematic (if subtle) deprivations and humiliations. . . . From the men on the bottom, with their injured will, the world gets rapists and muggers eager to give back to the world the violation and theft of dignity they have suffered.[15]

The next dramatic episode of father-son anguish, and in this case intended abuse, happens when Abraham, "the father of a great nation," obeys his Father-God, takes his only son, Isaac, whom he loved so much, and hikes up the mountain to sacrifice him as a burnt offering.

The same capricious God who rejected Cain's offering is now mandating that his trusted servant Abraham kill his precious offspring. Son Isaac shows utter faith in his father. He goes without qualms; "So the two of them went together." (22:6) This is surely one of the more plaintive lines in Old Testament lore.

God saves Isaac when he senses Abraham's unbending obedience, but the damage had been done. The cycle of violence, real or postponed, repeats itself across the male generations. The loyal father, driven by some higher vision, however twisted or debased, is willing to abuse, even destroy his innocent, treasured son. The love between the two is deep but distorted, as it often is between father and son.

Elie Wiesel amplifies:

There was no understanding the three characters. Why would God, the merciful Father, demand that Abraham become inhuman, and why would Abraham accept? And Isaac, why did he submit so meekly? [16]

Kirk Douglas in his autobiography, *The Ragman's Son,* recounts the torturous story of Abraham and Isaac and its effect upon his life as a Jewish child:

The Bible stories frightened me. Jehovah seemed such a cruel old man. I was afraid of him and didn't like him. A thought, needless to say, that I shared with no one. The picture from my Sunday school book is vivid in my mind. Abraham grasps his son Isaac in one arm; in the other he has a raised knife. He is remonstrating with the angel, who is trying to stop him from fulfilling God's commandment — "Sacrifice your son Isaac as a burnt offering to me." Isaac's eyes are open wide with fear. That little kid looked a lot like me. God had to come and help the angel and reassure Abraham that he was only testing him.

Now is that any way for a God to act? Don't you think he's taking advantage of his position? Don't you think he's cruel? Would my father use the knife that he cut holes in ragbags with to slit my throat if God asked him? It scared the hell out of me! [17]

Douglas already had a tormented, rage-filled relationship with his father. Such stories as Abraham and Isaac fueled the fire. Although a generation of new men are struggling to become the humane, intimate fathers they never had, all too often the terrorizing tale of torment, embodied in Abraham and Isaac, is re-enacted in households across the world.

This painful story cannot be easily dismissed. It starkly reminds us that the practice of human sacrifice has happened throughout history and still goes on in varying degrees and styles. Human sacrifices aren't reserved for the olden days alone. Our ways are equally pernicious and devastating — simply subtler and more "dignified."

Too many fathers sacrifice our young to the gods of war and patriotism, to our jobs, to our reputation, to our expectations and dreams, to our social commitments . . . to a whole host of "Almighties."

Our boss may ask us to go one step further in order to demonstrate our unyielding allegiance to the corporation or cause, and in our so doing, who invariably suffers? Who is sacrificed? Our children. Our Isaacs.

Additional notes on the Abraham-Isaac story. A Midrash account tells us that Isaac is not a youngster or even a youth, but a grown man of thirty-seven. This painfully demonstrates again how difficult it is for sons to grow to responsible maturity with our fathers. Isaac was nearly a mid-lifer and was still submissive to his Dad.

Isaac never quite outgrows the nightmare, for he repeats the sin of his forefathers in showing preferential treatment toward one of his twin sons, Esau.

However, it is touching that Isaac and his brother Ishmael buried their father in a cave, at the ripe old age of 175. Perhaps, as the two brothers carried out this meaningful and memorable act together, some peace was made between father and son at the time of Abraham's death.

And, of course, Isaac was blessed with his moniker. "Isaac" means "laughter." In his struggle to outgrow the primal father-son wound, he would need all the laughter he could muster, the remainder of his days.

Wailing Fathers

One more biblical example of father-son strife. David experienced a lifetime of upset and contentiousness with his rebellious son, Prince Absalom. In II Samuel 18:33 we witness one of the more plaintive male outbursts in all of literature. David weeps not only for the tragic death of his son but for his own failure as a father. He is wailing for what he never had in his severed relationship with his son Absalom. The grief-stricken David mourns uncontrollably: "O my son Absalom, my son, my son Absalom! Would I had died instead of you. O Absalom, my son, my son!"

Fathers throughout history join David in screaming lamentations for the sons they never knew, the sons they seldom affirmed, the sons they loved too late.

BROTHERS

Reconciling Twins

After looking at father-son dynamics we now turn to brothering engagements in the Old Testament. We start with the story of Esau and Jacob in Genesis 25:19.

The Bible relates that these brothers were already fighting inside their mother's womb — an omen of things to come. Although Esau and Jacob were twins, their lifestyles were radically dissimilar: hairy Esau was a hunter, a man of the field, whereas his younger brother Jacob was smooth, a tent-dweller, a homebody.

God announced that these sons would symbolize two rival nations, so it is no surprise that their relationship would prove to be a rocky, combative one.

Jacob was born with his hand on Esau's heel. Consequently he was called "the supplanter" or "the grabber," a name which he well resembled.

Parental favoritism aggravated matters: Isaac preferred Esau while Rebekah liked son Jacob. The lines were drawn early on; wedges inserted between mother and father, parents and sons.

One day Jacob tricks Esau into trading away his birthright, then years later he continues his deceitful ways by stealing Esau's blessing too. Jacob does this, with the collusion of his mother, by masquerading as his brother and winning the favor of his nearly blind, unsuspecting father Isaac. The "grabber" has undercut his twin twice.

Esau is furious and weeps as his father looks on helplessly. He sets out to slay his kin. Naturally, Jacob's conspirator in crime, Mother Rebekah, learns of Esau's plot and whisks Jacob off to Uncle Laban's house until Esau's rage is spent. Even at Laban's, Jacob continues his devious behavior.

It has always amused me that religious congregations end worship with the Old Testament benediction: "May the Lord watch between me and thee when we are absent one from another." This beautiful sounding pledge arose out of Laban's distrust for his son-in-law Jacob and called upon God to witness that Jacob not mistreat Laban's daughters or take other wives!

Unlike the Cain and Abel debacle, Esau and Jacob, after many years, are reunited. This story of reconciliation is one of the most powerful in the Bible, requiring time, distance, and especially Jacob's conversion — a new perspective born of his surprise discovery of Yahweh: "Surely, God was in this place and I did not know it." (Genesis 28:16) Jacob's repentance is matched by Esau's compassion.

Genesis 32 relates the story of healing. Jacob reaches out to Esau, informing him that he is now ready to return home, and hopes that his brother will be friendly. Messengers return with the news that Esau is on his way to meet Jacob, however with an army of 400 soldiers!

Jacob is frantic with fear, but instead of retreating, he turns to his God in prayer. Jacob confesses his unworthiness and calls upon God's support to carry him through. He has prepared his heart through sincere prayer.

Then he promises a present for his brother Esau: loads of animals to be given, he says, by the "servant Jacob" to "his master Esau!" His strategy is to appease Esau with gifts before meeting him face to face. The presents are sent on ahead. Jacob goes to sleep hoping that he will soon be reconciled with a friendly Esau.

That night occasions the greatest wrestling match in history. Jacob's foe is unclear: it could be a man, an angel, himself, or even God. Elie Wiesel says:

> This unknown, oddly behaved aggressor, who was he? Who had sent him? And for what purpose? Was he even a human being? The Biblical text uses the word *ish*, man. The Midrash and the commentators elevate him to the rank of angel. As for Jacob — who should have known — he situated him higher yet: *I have seen God face to face, yet my life has been preserved.* The aggressor readily confirmed this appraisal: Ki sarita im El — *Your name shall be Israel, for you fought God and you defeated Him.*[18]

In truth, his opponent matters not, for Jacob is engaged in a powerful, life-shaking struggle which alters his character forever.

Jacob emerges scathed yet triumphant after the awesome night-long fight: limping with a new name, "Israel." He called the place Peniel or "the face of God." For on his way to meet his brother face to face, Jacob has encountered his Creator face to face. Apparently, Jacob must make peace with God before doing likewise with his earthly kin.

Jacob becomes Israel, "the one who struggles or strives with God." Jacob, the deceitful grabber becomes a holy struggler. What's in a name? Everything. As a supplanter he was the one who had lied to his father and cheated his brother. He had been unfaithful to others and sabotaging to self. When he chose to become the one who strives with God, the new mandate was to grow truthful to his convictions, his loves, and his ongoing spiritual struggle as a brother.

However, the word "Israel" means more. It denotes, say the scholars, not only "he who strives with God" but also "God strives." We human beings are not alone in our striving. Universal energy — divine mystery, creative interchange — is also yearning, reaching out, and striving. The whole universe lies in agonizing yet concerned struggle. Jacob and God are partners . . . in striving.

After prayer, offering presents, and wrestling toward a new identity, Jacob is finally ready to be reconciled with his twin brother, his former foe.

"Far in the distance" Jacob sees Esau coming with his 400 men. Confident in his newfound serenity and religious identity, yet still unsure how Esau felt toward him, Jacob marches forward. As he approaches his brother he bows not once, not twice, but seven times, in deference and affection. Then Esau runs to meet his brother, embraces and kisses him, and both of them dissolve in tears.

Initially Esau turns Jacob's gifts down because he already has plenty. At this juncture, Esau addresses Jacob with the affectional term, "brother." (Genesis 33:9) Jacob insists, knowing that it is crucial for himself to be generous with Esau after he has been so demeaning. The gifts are a visible token of the invisible sacrament of healing between the brothers. "Please take my gifts. For God has been very generous to me, and I have enough." Finally, Esau accepts them.

Their peacemaking ritual is not complete. Esau reciprocates with his own kindness, offering men to assist Jacob as guides. Jacob, feeling secure, turns down Esau's gracious gesture.

They go their separate ways and this marvelous peacemaking encounter concludes with Jacob erecting an altar to the God of Israel.

The closing episode in their shared pilgrimage occurs when they join together (35:29) in burying their father, Isaac, whom they hold in common.

Esau and Jacob are born as fraternal twins, they separate through deceit and meanness, then re-brother because of the transforming power of repentance, compassion, and forgiveness.

Our brother stories need not end in disgrace and destruction. Our wounds can be healed, peace can be restored, and a legacy of love can be left behind. Esau and Jacob have shown all men how to reconcile.

Broken Brothers Heal

Until now our brothering situations have been dyadic. The next family context is more complex: it involves Joseph in relationship to one full brother and ten half-brothers.

Just as God favored Cain and Isaac favored Esau, so also Jacob favors Joseph.

> Now Israel loved Joseph more than any of his children,
> because he was the son of his old age: and he made him a
> long robe with sleeves. But when his brothers saw that
> their father loved him more than all his brothers, they
> hated him, and could not speak peaceably to him.
>
> — Genesis 37:3,4

Murderous instincts are passed along too. Just as Cain killed Abel and Esau sought to kill his brother Jacob, so Joseph's brothers seek to snuff him out.

Reuben wants to spare his brother's life; so he conceives the plan to throw Joseph alive into a well, so he can come back later and save him. There's often one sibling in each clan who goes against the group mood of vindictiveness.

Anyway, the brothers buy Reuben's plan because then Joseph would die in the well without their touching him. However, while Reuben is away, some traders come by, and the other brothers decide to sell Joseph to them: "Why kill him and have a guilty conscience? Let's not be responsible for his death, for, after all, he is our brother."

This transaction will salve their consciences plus garner some cash. Reuben weeps when he returns and realizes that Joseph is gone. The brothers spatter blood on Joseph's coat and take it to Jacob to identify. Joseph's father assumes that a wild animal has killed his favorite son, and he cries out in deepest mourning.

Joseph continues to be a favored man: by God, by Potiphar, a member of the personal staff of Pharaoh, and then by the chief jailer who turns over the entire prison administration to Joseph.

Joseph also becomes the pre-eminent dream-interpreter in Egypt and, ascending rapidly in power and status, later becomes a statesman. As governor of all Egypt and in charge of the sale of grain, Joseph's brothers come to him for famine relief and bow low before him, with their faces to the earth. Joseph recognizes them instantly, but pretends he doesn't.

Joseph is rough on his brothers. They claim to be brothers one to another while Joseph calls them spies. He challenges them to prove their identity by having one of their group stay in Egypt in prison while the rest go back to their father in Canaan, pick up the youngest brother and bring him back to Joseph.

Jacob is terror-stricken and exclaims to the sons: "You have bereaved me of my children: Joseph didn't come back, Simeon is gone, and now you want to take Benjamin too! Everything has been against me!" (42:36) Judah persuades his recalcitrant father to allow Benjamin to return with them. He guarantees his safety.

When the brothers arrive again in Egypt, Joseph gazes upon his youngest brother Benjamin and makes a hasty exit, for he is overcome with love for his brother. Going into his bedroom, Joseph weeps. Then he washes his face and comes out, keeping himself under control. They eat and have a merry time with wonderful bantering back and forth.

After one more attempt to fool his brothers by hiding his own silver cup in Benjamin's sack, Joseph can contain his feelings no longer. He reveals himself to his brothers in an avalanche of sobs.

They are stunned into silence. Joseph forgives his brothers, encouraging them not to be too hard on themselves. So often we need another family member to forgive us so that we might release ourselves from self-imposed shame and guilt.

Then weeping with joy, Joseph embraces Benjamin who starts to cry. There was a special bond between the two of them which endured through the separation of nearly twenty years. Then Joseph embraces each of the other brothers, who finally find their tongues. When reconciliation occurs in our lives, we men can break *our* silence, *our* voices can return.

Joseph lavishes new clothes upon his kin. Pharaoh assigns them the best territories in the land of Egypt. All is well, very well. Yet Joseph makes a parting plea: "Don't quarrel along the way!" (45:24) Joseph exhorts his brothers to honor their common family and remember their reunion by treating one another lovingly. Now is not the time to wreck what has been restored.

The brothers return and Jacob cries out: "Joseph my son is alive! I will go and see him before I die." The family moves to Egypt.

Then comes the blessing. The cruciality of men receiving a blessing in their formative years is noted by contemporary Jungian philosopher Robert Moore:

> Being blessed has tremendous psychological consequences for us. There are even studies that show that our bodies actually change chemically when we feel valued, praised, and blessed.
>
> Young men today are starving for blessing from older men, starving for blessing from the King energy. This is why they cannot, as we say, "get it together." They shouldn't have to. They need to be blessed.[19]

On his deathbed, Jacob blesses his sons, "Blessing each with the blessing suitable to him." (49:28) When he finishes his blessing, Jacob lies back in bed, breathes his last, and dies in peace.

But at their father's funeral, an unsteady peace prevails as the brothers grow anxious that Joseph may be vengeful toward them and they beg for his forgiveness. Joseph, the most tear-prone man in religious history, breaks down yet again, allays their fears, and reassures them that he forgives all and will take good care of them.

The healing is mutual and complete when the brothers together promise Joseph that, upon his death, they will take him back to Canaan, their homeland.

Healing brokenness among brothers is a holy event and its importance cannot be overemphasized. The male-to-male link is a democratic one that, when restored, allows men to live freer, fuller lives.

These brothering stories from Genesis of intrigue, guilt, betrayal, repentance, and reconciliation remind men that we are challenged to make peace on earth with divinity *and* with fellow humans. When Jacob concludes his wrestling with God, his opponent is moved to say: "Your name shall no more be called Jacob, but Israel, for you have striven with God and with men, and have prevailed." (Genesis 32:28)

When we reconcile or bond with God — for whatever reasons, in whatever kind of struggle — we are spiritually prepared to do likewise with our brothers and sisters. The converse is also true: when we deepen or heal bonds with our neighbors, we are preparing the way for the same reconciliation with God. Horizontal and vertical reconciliation are mutually reinforcing.

Teammates on a Shared Mission

> Behold, how good and pleasant it is when brothers dwell together in unity! It is like the precious oil upon the head, running down upon the beard of Aaron, running down on the collar of his robes!
>
> — Psalm 133:1,2

Moses and Aaron take brothering to a new level. These brothers major in the craft of teamwork. They are partners.

Each had his own gifts. Aaron was the orator, Moses was the leader. Aaron displayed weakness of will when he gave in to the people's clamor for a golden calf. Moses could be a hothead.

The beauty of their brothering is the separation of duties. Moses would receive a task from God, and the eloquent Aaron would deliver the news to the people. They functioned as a team. They were the first biblical brothers to appreciate their differences as strengths to be utilized rather than weaknesses to be exploited. They were happy for each other too. Wiesel notes: "Only once do we see Moses joyous: on the day his brother Aaron acceded to the office of high priest." [20]

It doesn't matter that one (Moses) was in the foreground and the other (Aaron) was invariably in the background, because both were essential, critical to accomplish the shared mission. "Shared" is the word because they are usually mentioned together in the book of Exodus. Alone they are adequate; together they are mighty.

Lest we romanticize these siblings, there are awkward and jealous times as well. Aaron once joined their sister in criticism of Moses. And the latter got angry at Aaron upon more than one occasion (cf. Chapter 32).

I can personally identify with Aaron and Moses because my father had only one sibling and so do I. Within each pair — Wilber and Harold, Phil and Tom — three years of age separate the brothers, just like with Moses and Aaron.

As brothers we bank upon one another because we are all we have. We are close enough in age not to be out of touch with one another. My brother, the psychotherapist, and I, the minister, share a profound and common vision of existence. Our task is not as awesome as bringing the Decalogue to the people, but we do good work alongside one another. We are teammates.

Chosen Brothers, Friends Forever

We observe another variation of brothering in David and Jonathan, who were not blood kin but chosen brothers. Their love-bond goes down in religious literature as one of the strongest between two persons, married or not, male or female.

Scriptural passages attest to the depth and power of their bond.

> The soul of Jonathan was knit to the soul of David, and Jonathan loved him as his own soul. . . . Then Jonathan made a covenant with David, because he loved him as much as his own soul. And Jonathan stripped himself of the robe that was upon him, and gave it to David, and his armor, and even his sword and his bow and his girdle.
>
> — I Samuel 18:1-4

They seal their covenant with gifts.

> But Jonathan made David swear to it again, this time by his love for him, for he loved him as much as he loved himself.
>
> — I Samuel 20:17

This rephrasing of the second great commandment in both the Old and New Testaments — to love thy neighbor as thyself — is vivid evidence of their unceasing affection.

In David's dirge composed for Saul and Jonathan is found this beautiful sentiment:

> I am distressed for you, my brother Jonathan; very pleasant have you been to me; your love to me was wonderful, passing the love of women.
>
> — II Samuel 1:26

In this crowning ode to their friendship, David claims that their reciprocated love outsoars any of the relationships he has had with women. This passage is reminiscent of the power of male-bonding in war literature. As Philip Caputo said in *A Rumor of War:*

> Communion between men (in infantry battalions) is as profound as any between lovers. Actually it is more so. . . . It is, unlike marriage, a bond that cannot be broken by a word, by boredom or divorce, or by anything other than death. Sometimes that is not strong enough.[21]

Or as is stated in the movie *Beau Geste:* "Love of man for woman waxes and wanes. Love of brother for brother is steadfast as the stars."[22]

Whether Jonathan and David's friendship was also sexual or not, we will never know. It does demonstrate that a loving devoted tie between men or women can be prized as the highest and holiest affection we know. Such was the case with David and Jonathan.

It was a remarkable friendship when you weigh the odds. There were vast differences in their social and economic backgrounds. James Auchmuty compares them in his book, *Brothers of the Bible:*

> Jonathan was accustomed to the active social life and privileges that belonged to the nation's first family and were his as eldest son of the king. David, on the other hand, was a study in contrasts. He was the youngest son of a farmer, a shepherd who enjoyed the solitude that was his under the big sky of Palestinian pastures. His bunk in an animal hide tent or in a dark cave was hardly comparable to the prince's chamber in the ruler's palace. And David's name was not even on the ballot when Samuel, the prophet, came by to vote on God's choice as Saul's successor.[23]

There was no rational basis for a budding friendship between this improbable pair, yet they meshed.

They were bonded in devotion: "Tell me what I can do," says Jonathan (I Samuel 20:4). They kissed one another, cried together (20:41). They entrusted their future and that of their children into God's hands forever (20:42).

Their friendship endured through difficult tests of trust and bravery. They were bonded in danger. Indeed Jonathan narrowly escaped his own death as well as that of his friend, David, both at the hands of Jonathan's crazed father, King Saul.

Remember that Jonathan was devoted to David even though he knew that David, not himself, would become the King. Few men would agree to play second fiddle to their friend.

Theirs was not another starry-eyed friendship but one which weathered storms and obstacles.

David and Jonathan enjoyed a tie which embodied the essence of the Proverbs passage: "There are friends who pretend to be friends, but there is a friend who sticks closer than a brother." (Proverbs 18:24) They didn't need to stick closer than a brother; they were brothers — forever.

Our Elder Brother

It would be fascinating to track the various interactions (the call, the companionship, the mission, the betrayal, the death, the resurrection) between Jesus and his disciples, followers, and figures such as John the Baptist, but that's not the goal of this book.

It is also worthwhile to note that Jesus evidently felt closer to his *chosen* family than his *biological* one:

> Now his mother and brothers arrived at the crowded house where Jesus was teaching, and they sent word for him to come out and talk with them. "Your mother and brothers are outside and want to see you," he was told. Jesus replied, "Who is my mother? Who are my brothers?" Looking at those around him, he said, "These are my mother and brothers! Anyone who does God's will is my brother, and my sister, and my mother."
>
> — Mark 3:31-35

I want us to view Jesus as our peer, in a horizontal, democratic relationship rather than in an hierarchical fashion where he is the Son of God, heavenly father, and savior. One of my favorite holiday carols is the medieval French song called "The Friendly Beasts," one of the verses of which reads:

> Jesus, our brother kind and good,
> Was humbly born in a stable rude,
> And the friendly beasts around him stood;
> Jesus, our brother kind and good.
> "I," said the donkey, shaggy and brown,
> "I carried his mother up hill and down,
> I carried his mother to Bethlehem town.
> I," said the donkey, shaggy and brown . . .

If the animals can treat the Galilean as their brother, so can we humans. Whatever else we might choose to call Jesus, "brother" surely must be one of the namings if we men are to make progress on our Brother-Spirit journey.

Kenneth Patton, minister and poet, describes how Jesus evolved from "the perfect creature," "very God himself" to "Jesus my friend, my companion, my brother . . . " along Patton's own spiritual odyssey:

The Man Jesus

> Jesus, you were the man of my vision and dreaming;
> you were the perfect creature without stain or blemish,
>   the never sinning, the unmistaken, the all-loving, the
>   all-knowing;
> you were the end of creation, the fullest and completest
>   point in history and time;
> you were the goal, the apex, the unattainable being, very
>   God himself.
> Jesus, you were the beacon light to my spirit, the anchor
>   of my hope, the searchlight in the darkness leading
>   me;
> you were my hero, my guide, my teacher, the not-to-be-
>   questioned, the gladly accepted, saviour, redeemer,
>   friend.
> Unto you, Jesus, did I cling even when I rejected your
>   father, God himself.
> You were still perfect man when perfect god was gone.
> You were the last rock to which I clung in the sea of flux
>   and change.

> You were the last to walk the tossing waters and not to
> sink therein.
> Yet there was that within me which would not permit
> you, Jesus, to walk alone, the perfect one in a world
> of imperfection.
> There was that within me which could not hold forever
> onto you, that forced me to shove off from you to
> swim by myself in the sea.
> For there grew within me the knowledge that you too
> were but a swimmer in the sea, and that the sea at
> last closed over you, as it will one day close over me.
> I have lost you, Jesus my idol, the unscalable mountain,
> my God.
> But I have found you again, Jesus my friend, my
> companion, my brother, who once dreamed even as
> now I dream, who lost as I shall lose, who died as I
> shall die.[24]

One of the most telling encounters of brothering in the New Testament transpires when Jesus has dinner with his disciples at the Passover meal (John 13). Remember that "companionship" literally means those who eat together.

At this last supper Jesus washes the disciples' feet, then mandates them to wash the feet of one another. Through this act of servanthood Jesus is declaring that the litmus test of the religious leader is whether they can have friends, not only followers. His disciples are his friends.

Jesus believes in peer-to-peer compassion rather than master-servant, guru-devotee kinship. He identifies with his closest buddies and stoops to wash their feet. Later in the evening he says:

> A new commandment I give to you, that you love one
> another; even as I have loved you, that you also love one
> another. By this all people will know that you are my
> disciples, if you have love for one another.
>
> — John 13:34-35

Jesus proceeds to say more about love for his disciples, his friends, his brothers:

> Greater love has no one than this, that a person lays
> down his life for his friends. You are my friends if you do
> what I command you. No longer do I call you servants,

for the servant does not know what the master is doing,
but I have called you friends, for all that I have heard
from my Father I have made known to you.

— John 15:13-15

So brotherly love is the crowning invitation of Jesus' ministry —
not subservience, not conquest, not acquisition, not glory, but a
profound compassion which reaches across, man-to-man, to wash,
to caress, to embrace our neighbors.

The consummate lover of humanity encourages us to go and do
likewise. He dies with the hope that his brotherly spirit will live on
in the compassion of his friends. Such is our brothering path.

A FAMILY OF MEN

The title Prodigal Son doesn't do justice to this parable (Luke 15:11-32). First, it is not the story of one son but the complex interplay between a father and two sons. It is also the episode about a younger and older brother. It explores multiple relationships. Second, the one son may be prodigal in his wasteful living but the other is overly frugal in his demonstration of feeling. Perhaps the most prodigal, lavish display is the outpouring of unmerited affection shown by the father first to his wayward younger son, then to his recalcitrant older son.

It is traditional to interpret this parable metaphorically and see it strictly as an example of God's gracious forgiveness in the face of our sinful, squandering behavior. While it remains a powerful display of divine forgiveness, I want to explore the inter-familial, male-male dimensions of the story which are so humanly portrayed. As a parable of hurt, healing, alienation, and hope, it can help guide our Brother-Spirit quest for greater intimacy and ultimacy.

The younger brother isn't greedy because he asks simply for his fair share of the estate. But his timing shows disrespect. All of the sons we have analyzed in Old Testament families at least return upon their father's death to pay homage. By taking off early, and going to a distant land, there is little assurance that the younger son will be present at the close of his father's life.

He is self-centered, thinking neither of father nor brother. He personifies narcissism.

In a few short verses his existence turns from good to bad to lousy. He wastes all — not a portion — of his money on parties and prostitutes. He is a *prodigal* son.

Then he has sufficient presence of mind (or is it hunger of stomach) to persuade a local farmer to hire him to feed his pigs. He isn't afraid to work or too proud to eat with the swine.

"And no one gave him anything." (v. 16) There was no human mercy shown, no good Samaritan in the wings to rescue this prodigal son.

"When he finally comes to his senses," (v. 17) the younger brother exhibits a person in trouble willing to turn his life around. The first step in repentance is facing yourself head on: your flaws, misdeeds, and poverties.

Some commentators are distrustful of the younger brother's rapid conversion. They think he was drawn more by desperation than a genuine change of heart. It doesn't matter, does it? When we turn within, face our wrongs, prepare our confession, we are inexorably on the road to recovery.

I am impressed that he is ready to declare his sin "against both heaven *and* you" (v. 18) and his willingness to forfeit his sonship and become a hired hand.

Those are not insincere gestures, however dire his straits are. He was not one for idle daydreaming. The younger brother acted; "he arose and came to his father." (v. 20) He humbled himself.

"And while he was still a long distance away, his father saw him coming, and was filled with loving pity and ran and embraced him and kissed him." (15:20) That is my single favorite verse in the entire Judeo-Christian scriptures. As Reinhold Niehbuhr stated: "Forgiveness is the final form of love," and here is the most visible showering of forgiveness imaginable. No questions are asked, no conditions are required, no time is wasted — in fact, no words are even offered. Only actions.

An onslaught of caring verbs follows: *"Saw* him coming," *"was filled* with loving pity," *"ran,"* *"embraced* him," and *"kissed* him." Love is an active force not a passive substance, a verb rather than a noun. The father embodies that wisdom.

The father did this while the son "was still a long distance away." He just couldn't wait. He couldn't contain his love. He raced out to meet his lost, now found son; his dead, now alive son. My hunch is that the father was on the lookout everyday, so it comes as no surprise that he saw him arriving home that morning.

The son starts in to confess his sin and is cut short, midway through the litany, because the prodigal father can't wait to lavish material gifts upon his son, after first lavishing him with spiritual love.

The son turned around, and the father turned toward him. The necessary movements for forgiveness are born. The son's effort and the father's grace together create the gift of forgiveness.

Ample kisses, the finest robe, jeweled ring, shoes, and then the feast. Reconciliation always needs a celebration.

The older brother is livid upon hearing of the celebration. He refuses to attend.

The ever generous, gracious father begs him to join the festivities. He isn't interested in leaving out anyone, certainly not the other son whom he loves.

The older brother balks, then rails at his father for never throwing parties like this for him and his friends, even though he has unfailingly done his job all his adult life. He acidly labels his brother, "this son of yours," disavowing any connection with the squanderer. Whereas Cain killed Abel, the older brother here spiritually cancels his kin.

The faithful son is logical and accurate but is clamoring for justice in a situation which cries out for mercy. Love transcends fairness. The father caringly says:

> Son, you are always with me, and all that is mine is yours.
> It was fitting to make merry and be glad, for this your
> brother was dead, and is alive; he was lost, and is found.
> (15:31-32)

The prodigal father has room and love in his heart for both sons. He has broken the paternal pattern of showing preferential treatment in biblical families; he refuses to play favorites. Both sons are precious to him. He reminds the older son that "he is your brother," a bond not to be denied or severed but affirmed and celebrated.

It is right to celebrate. Everyone is welcome.

What is most revealing about this parable is the unconditional forgiveness shown between father and son. It is the quintessential homecoming story which heals father-son wounds for all men everywhere.

What is most haunting about this story is its incompleteness. The younger brother heals within himself and with his father. But the older brother is a hold-out. He is unwilling to forgive. He shuts himself out of the celebration. The parable ends with a partial party. Not everyone is there.

We could well rename the episode the "Parable of the Vengeful Son." As James Auchmuty writes:

> A certain man had two sons: one strayed, the other stayed. One broke his father's heart, the other never understood his father's heart. The sin of son was rooted in passion; the sin of the other was rooted in disposition. One was guilty of sins of the flesh; the other was guilty of sins of the spirit. The sin of one was open, the sin of the other was secret. One never intended to hurt anyone; the other never intended to help anyone. One tried to enjoy everything; the other could enjoy nothing. One said, "I must change"; the other said, "I have no need of change, and those who need change, cannot."
>
> When the story ends, the boy who had remained near his father's house was outside. And he who had run away was inside.[25]

The older brother was entitled to two-thirds of the estate, simply by virtue of seniority, while his kin took off with only one-third. The elder brother had small reason to squawk.

Men were needed to stay home in an agrarian society, and he had done so. He had served his family admirably. He could be proud of his devotion and accomplishments. He was cherished and loved by his father. He would not diminish in stature if he chose to applaud his brother's return. Indeed, his spiritual size would enlarge with such a generous move. But he chooses the way of scorn and self-righteousness.

All is not lost, for his father goes back out to get him and re-welcome him into the family celebration. The father didn't give up on his younger son; he won't with the older one either. His invitation still holds, so does his love. Come in, my son, give up your sanctimonious smugness and return home by joining the party.

Ann James offers:

> Only then, without a proper ending and with the pleas unanswered, does Jesus stop the story. Did the elder brother stay outside or did he repent and go in? It is up to the "elder brothers" — the Pharisees and those who have never strayed — to decide. Will we let go of the self-preserving distinctions that distance us from others and from God? Will we let go and live joyfully, celebrating

the bonds we share? Will we be like our elder brother, Jesus, who sat down at table with anyone — sinners, Pharisees, even the person who would betray him — because he knew that, as important as the standards that distinguish the righteous and the unrighteous may be, God's primary standard is love.[26]

The question still holds. The father still waits. The party is still going on.

JOURNEY

The deep, nourishing and spiritually radiant energy of the
male lies not in the feminine side, but in the deep
masculine. . . . The kind of energy I'm talking about is not
the same as macho brute strength . . . it's forceful action
undertaken, not with compassion, but with resolve.[1]

— Robert Bly

THE SACRED QUEST

The first section of this book explicated brothering examples in
the Bible, showing how men have wrestled in their male relationships, especially father-son and brother-brother encounters, as we try
to create heightened intimacy.

This second section centers upon the spiritual journey of men.
For some men the spirit awaits birth; for others it lives vigorously
and grows rapidly. Each brother travels at his own pace, along his
own path. Some of us are spiritual infants, others teens, a few are
adults. For each of us, the spiritual journey takes us toward a greater
appreciation of ultimacy. As Jesus is reported to have said in the
Gnostic Gospels:

If you bring forth what is within you, what is within you
will save you. If you do not bring forth what is within
you, what is within you will destroy you.

Whether we call this spiritual enthusiasm "deep masculine" (Robert Bly), "metaphysical hunger" (Sam Keen), "mature masculine" (Robert Moore), or "Brother-Spirit," it is clear that open, growing men are on an unmistakably sacred quest.

We have been evolving during the last two decades of the men's movement. I like the word movement because it denotes motion, growth, and change. Our progression has taken men from being reactive to women's liberation to being proactive for our own emancipation, from being focused on our achievements, then our feelings, and now our aspirations.

Emotional maturity is critical in our evolution as men, but we dare not stop there. Our spiritual wellness is also at stake. As a colleague of mine remarked: "Spiritual fulfillment is an evolutionary mandate for us men."

Men are now interested in migrating from emotional sharing to spiritual questing, from venting our spleens to venturing our souls. As A. Powell Davies reminds us: "The purpose of life is to grow a soul." Women have realized this for decades, with their burgeoning religious energy and pathways. We men are coming of age too. John Sanford states in his book, *What Men Are Like:*

> Since our time in history is heavily extraverted, many men will find that they must now turn inward, and develop their introverted life. The prophet Elijah is an example. In the Israel of Elijah's time, the true worshippers of Yahweh had been banished and his enemy, Queen Jezebel, plotted to take his life. Discouraged and exhausted, Elijah went on a long pilgrimage across the desert to Mount Sinai. There he crept into a cave on the flank of the mountain and waited for God to speak to him. At last God spoke in a still, small voice. Out of the ensuing dialogue, Elijah got fresh courage and energy for his life, and returned to his task in Israel. This is a story of making a journey inward, of finding out that God speaks from the inmost soul.[2]

In my counseling with men as a minister, in my immersion in men's discussions, support groups, retreats and conferences, I hear concerns voiced like:

— "I have *done* much; I then learned how to *feel* deeply; I am interested today in *being* my real self. I am interested in matters of the soul."

— "Now that I am fairly freed up emotionally, what's next? Freedom is great, but I seek fulfillment."

— "I was reading Henry David Thoreau the other day and I realized what I want. I agree with him: 'To affect the quality of the day, that is the highest of the arts . . . I wish to live deliberately, to front only the essential facts of life. I wish to learn what life has to teach, and not, when I come to die, discover that I have not lived.' "

— "What does my life really add up to, now that I've reached middle age? As John Steinbeck asked, so do I: 'What have I contributed to the Great Ledger? What am I worth?' "

It used to be said of men that if the Holy Spirit itself burst into one of our gatherings like a lightning bolt we would probably miss it, ignore it, or analyze it rather than experience or exult in it. Not so anymore.

While maintaining our commitment to intellectual integrity, we are increasingly open to the presence and power of spirituality. I believe that we become more whole and robust men when we move beyond excessive rationalism, activism, and scientism. We need to be a spirited, exuberant, inspirational (which literally means "to breathe life into") gender for our own good and the good of all whom we meet along the path.

The following scenarios present themselves:

— Our physical burdens and emotional problems as men remain, yet spiritual desires capture most of our current attention.

— Men participate in professional management seminars to advance our vocational skills, but new expertise doesn't ease our deep-down aches.

— We are involved in relationship growth workshops which enhance our intimacy level with self, women, and other men but leave issues of ultimacy untouched.

In the life-long sweep of the Brother-Spirit journey, men have only begun. It is no longer enough for us to cook, talk, weep, and camp together, as cathartic and cementing as those ventures are. Our major quest is a spiritual one. In order to be whole persons we must engage the agonies and ecstasies of the sacred journey both alone and alongside our brothers.

A fragment from one of Rainer Maria Rilke's poems reads:

> Sometimes a man stands up during supper and walks outside, and keeps on walking, because of a church that stands somewhere in the East.[3]

Men are standing up during dinners everywhere, walking outside toward that far-flung, yet fulfilling, vision in the East — the vision of spiritual sustenance, the vision of genuine, durable hope, the vision of some purpose beyond power, a quest beyond the expression of body or emotion alone.

What Is Spirituality?

This section will describe spirituality, clarify some of its dangers and benefits, then pinpoint what makes Brother-Spirit a distinct venture from either the monastic movement or contemporary feminist religion. One caveat. I know that the following introductory comments on spirituality may apply to the purposes of both women and men, but I compose them as a male primarily for men's eyes and hearts.

What does spirituality mean? There is no definitive description of spirituality available, although there are some religious clans who try to package it on lampshades, slogans, pamphlets, and bumper stickers.

The Spirit/spirit can be caught occasionally but never captured. "The wind blows where it wills, and you hear the sound of it, but you do not know whence it comes or whither it goes; so it is with every one who is born of the Spirit." (John 3:8) I have found that when we least expect it, the spirit sneaks or crashes into our existence.

At a Midwest conference I led on Brother-Spirit, I started by asking the men what phrases came to mind when I mentioned the word: "spirituality." Here are some of their replies:

— seeing beyond walls

— an internal caress

— essence

— communion with God

— getting out of my own way

— time of deepest doubt

— true sexual union

— beauty

— the willing suspension of disbelief

— listening to my higher consciousness

— experiencing profound trust

— growth through adversity

— alone in nature

— sense of self as mysterious

— feeling integral to the whole universe

— being fully alive

I added the basic, literal meaning of *spiritus:* breath or wind. Therefore, we are spirited or spiritual when we catch our breath, when we receive surprise, graceful second winds during the course of our daily skirmishes and pursuits.

However we attempt to define "spirituality," the truth remains: we can dull and blunt the spirit but we cannot eradicate it. It is undeniable. It is a presence and force which comes and goes in human life. There is a chant which runs: "You can't kill the spirit, it's like the ocean, on and on, it goes on and on . . . " I often sing that as a meditative anchor in my daily grind.

Visiting our "interior castles," as called by St. Theresa of Avila, is no easy trek in a culture which mass-produces external gurus. The sacred quest is like the woman who approached a Zen master to ascertain final directions. She blurts out: "I have come to learn the path. I have come to learn the path." The Zen master, silent for a moment, points to her with loving intensity and says: "You are the path! You are the path!"

There may be guides and veterans to share our Brother-Spirit quest, but there are no carriers, let alone rescuers. As the old gospel song relates: "Jesus walked this lonesome valley. He had to walk it by himself. Oh, nobody else could walk it for him. He had to walk it by himself." And verse two proceeds: "We must walk this lonesome valley. We have to walk it by ourselves . . . "

Robert Bly writes in his introduction to *The Kabir Book:*

> To Kabir, the fifteenth century Sufi and Hindu master
> and poet, the main danger is spiritual passivity. Kabir is
> opposed to repeating any truth from another teacher,
> whether of English literature or Buddhism, that you
> yourself have not experienced.[4]

The ways of spirituality are manifold. I grow weary of gurus peddling their spiritual discipline as the only way to inner truth and serenity. There are many disciplines. The routes are plural. There are spiritualities.

Vern Curry phrases it aptly:

> As the words we use differ, the paths we follow differ.
> Think of these differences this way. We each begin, as it
> were, on the rim of a wheel. Travelling by the spoke
> nearest our position we move toward a common center or
> hub. As we approach the hub, each spoke is nearer to
> another. Differences, large at first at the rim, diminish as
> we approach the center.[5]

In short, different spokes for different folks!

The devices used to bring about our spiritual state are as diverse as gazing quietly at a candle flame, attending to the mental repetition of a mantra, following one's own breathing, chanting out loud a phrase from a song, listening to bodily sensations, whirling in dance, reading sentiments from a daily devotional, focusing on an unanswerable riddle.

The key thing, according to Carlos Castenada, is to choose a path with a heart. So the question for men is: does my spiritual path bring me greater intimacy with self and greater caring for neighbor and earth? And sometimes our paths will lose heart. When they do, there is no shame in dropping the path and pursuing an alternative one.

Whatever spiritual paths we men choose, all share one quality in common: "Grace is proportionate to exertion!" (Sathya Sai Baba) The spiritual fallacy of our modern era is that enduring enlightenment can be purchased for a price or garnered with minimal effort. The drop-out rate among meditators, for example, is great because devotees want shots of grace for the asking. How many people are still doing TM a decade later?

The reality is that while at first a spiritual discipline may bring mild highs or some relief from stress, there will come a time, as in the development of any sophisticated skill, when there will be a plateau. We may get bored, discouraged, negative, and cynical.

Then we separate the plodders from the enthusiasts, the men from the boys. If we loathe times of dryness and staleness, then we ought to stay away from spiritual practices because they are filled with deserts. The spiritual life is not for softies with little staying power.

As Catholic theologian Henri J. M. Nouwen writes:

> To live a spiritual life we must first find the courage to
> enter into the desert of loneliness and change it by gentle
> and persistent efforts into a garden of solitude.[6]

In whatever spiritual activity we engage, men need to avoid crash programs; we must mistrust the promise of quick fixes, ecstatic pleasures, and easy self-transformation. Instead, our effort should be to stay with a sensible, integrated, and self-tailored process of centering for as long as it fits. And we will be surprised and disappointed, and surprised again. But spiritual muscles do grow, tone, become more trim and supple. Just not overnight.

Dangers Along the Path

This Columbus-like voyage to our interior castles sounds enchanting to us men, yet there are lurking dangers and dragons.

First, sometimes we can be too zealous or goal oriented in our Brother-Spirit journey. The harder we try to be spiritually awake, the more we doze off. The resolution to this quandary is stated in Zen with infuriating simplicity: "Quit trying. Quit trying not to try. Quit quitting." And so it goes.

A second obstacle appears in the guise of spiritual materialism. We turn our spiritual journey into another acquisition, like a new car or TV set. The antidote to this familiar male addiction is for us not to make a big deal of our spiritual practice. Take it easy, wear it lightly. Don't dramatize your efforts, don't try to peddle your practice. Treat it as a flexible process rather than a shiny, new toy.

The Oriental wisdom relates: "The sage does not talk, the talented ones talk, and the stupid ones argue."

A third roadblock to sustained spiritual discipline is simply getting underway. Physical exercise specialists know that it is the first push-up rather than the last one that does the most good. The long journey begins with one step.

Benefits of Spiritual Discipline

Men usually ask: "What's in it for me? What are the benefits to be gained from a spiritually alive existence?" Americans are pragmatists and are skeptical about doing something without the prospect of positive results, so let me enumerate some of the benefits of the inward journey.

First, spiritual discipline is an opportunity to stop thinking and talking compulsively, as men are wont to do. It is a chance to cease the incessant clatter in our skulls and to listen to the subtle sounds of our interior homes.

Second, spirituality is a powerful process by which we come to feel our basic kinship with and inseparability from the interdependent web of the cosmos.

Third, spiritual discipline is an economic and effective use of our time to handle the stresses and pressures of daily existence. Many brothers find that taking mere moments out each day to reflect, ponder, be quiet, or meditate can produce a sufficient supply of serenity.

Fourth, the physical and emotional benefits are well documented. Spiritual centering relaxes us, reduces tension and need for sleep, induces tranquility, and increases sensory enjoyment. Colors are more vivid and music sounds fuller. Harry Meserve in *The Practical Meditator* writes: "We do not gain any more time for living, but we live a lot more, because our senses are much more alive and open to impressions from the world around us." [7] Strangely, we are both more peaceful and more awake.

Fifth, spirituality is not an alternative to political awareness. Real centeredness makes us less aggressive and energizes compassion. As my friend says, "We men don't have to use other people for our own ends when we possess interior repose."

Admittedly, for some men, Brother-Spirit can be a moral cop-out. It tranquilizes them into avoiding social responsibility. But all religious leaders like Mohammed and Dorothy Day, Buddha and Julian of Norwich were contemplatives and prophets. They balanced inner and outer lives. They knew that a "sound person's heart dare not be shut up within itself." (Tao)

The great religious pioneers have always believed that their spiritual discipline was never complete until someone else felt more loved by them. Our sacred quest as men should strengthen us for service. It should awaken us to what Zen master Thich Nhat Hanh declared the task of "looking at all beings with the eyes of compassion."

Gandhi brought together spiritual life and social witness in this way. He tried to meditate and always remember God, even in the thick of a crisis. When he was assassinated, his last words were the name of God.

Sixth, spirituality reminds us that we are bathed in mystery. Let those men who remain convinced that we can explain or control life sit for but ten minutes in absolute stillness and their sense of omnipotence will be destroyed.

Finally, spiritual discipline enables us to contribute meaning and power back to the vitality of the universe which brought us into being. As Meserve states it: "Many a little life has added something to the total of the eternal years. Good meditation is a method of repeating the natural miracle of returning life within the human mind and spirit." [8]

Two closing reminders for men as we undertake the spiritual life. First, spirituality is not a five-minute or even three-hour daily practice. It is a way of being in the universe, a way of life. Second, there is a distinction I make between spiritual friends, whom we need, and spiritual technicians, whom we don't. We need fellow-travelers rather than gurus.

Brother-Spirit and the Monastic Movement

There are several ways in which the Brother-Spirit and monastic movements differ.

First, men engaged in Brother-Spirit are encouraged to retreat for periodic renewal not ongoing seclusion. When our men's fellowship goes on its semi-annual weekends to the mountains, we call them renewals rather than retreats because we do not wish to imply that we are withdrawing from our family commitments or work stations.

I appreciate the term "retreat" because I believe it is crucial for men to seize respites from daily routine and pressure. I also understand the consensus viewpoint of my brothers who want our times apart and away to be advances not retreats, times of restoration not isolation.

Second, Brother-Spirit practices participatory democracy in its methods and relations, whereas the monastic movement is essentially hierarchical. Sometimes the first Christian hermits, back in the fourth century, were democratic as Thomas Merton notes:

> The Desert Fathers declined to be ruled by men, but had no desire to rule over others themselves. Nor did they fly from human fellowship. The society they sought in the deserts of Egypt, Arabia, and Palestine was one where all men were truly equal, where the only authority under God was the charismatic authority of wisdom, experience, and love. Of course, they acknowledged the benevolent, hierarchical authority of their bishops, but the bishops were far away and said little about what went on in the desert until the great Origenist conflict at the end of the fourth century.[9]

Brother-Spirit does not promote a clan, a cult, or a church but a collection of like-spirited men committed to the life-long quest for intimacy and ultimacy in our lives, whether at work, at home, or away in the mountains or desert. We call ourselves brothers not fathers, peers not patriarchs.

Third, while monks are destined to be *saints,* brothers settle for becoming *sages.*

Traditionally, sainthood was reserved for the dead. Progressive Catholic thought would acknowledge saints while on earth by the quality of their lives. Mother Theresa, Dorothy Day, and Thomas Merton are contemporary examples of religious persons who were truly "saints" on earth. Men in Brother-Spirit resonate with the sentiment of Dorothy Day:

> That's the way people try to dismiss you. If you're a saint, then you must be impractical and utopian, and nobody has to pay any attention to you. That kind of talk makes me sick.[10]

Why do brothers use the term "sage" to refer to one another? Sage means wise man; its female counterpart is "krone." Sages are those men who rise up from our midst, periodically, and speak compelling and compassionate truths. They are not holier than the rest. They do not separate themselves from the community. They aren't *always* brilliant, sagacious, or insightful. But *often* they are.

All men can become sages. It is our privilege, our call, our challenge.

Fourth, monks engage in purification while brothers pursue fulfillment. When one reads the moving testimony of such spiritual forebrothers as the Spanish mystic, St. John of the Cross (1542-1591), in his classic devotional tract, *Dark Night of the Soul,* his aim is clear: the active stripping of the soul of any imperfections and preparing it for union with God. It is nothing less than a whole-hearted, self-abnegating process of purgation.

I wouldn't claim that the Brother-Spirit process is without anguish and struggle, for we brothers are religious heirs of Jacob. We are frail and flawed; we must wrestle alone, all night long, with God if we are to emerge with a profound religious identity, our own spiritual name. Yet the focus and rigor of our sacred quest is markedly distinct from that of traditional monks.

We brothers follow the path of the Buddha, whose faith of the middle way encourages us to learn the arts of sensitive engagement and healthy detachment, of gentle holding and timely letting go.

Life enhancement rather than mortification is our goal. We are devoted to greater not lesser enjoyment of this earthly creation. We pay homage to the monks even as we part company.

Brother-Spirit and Feminist Religion

> Knowing the male but keeping the female, one becomes a universal stream. Becoming a universal stream, one is not separated from eternal virtue.[11]
>
> — Tao-Te-Ching

Feminist religious thought is complex, diverse, and rich. Women have created their own theology center, composed readings and memorial services for women, written trenchant journals, books, and songs, held retreats and festivals, and generated an authentically fresh and feminist-grounded faith in "paganism." Feminist religion is intensive, experiential, and spreading. In the Western world, Catholic, Jewish, and Protestant women are equally enmeshed in the creative edges of spiritual direction.

The scope of feminist religion is demonstrated in the variant titles women use to describe their work: "womanspirit," "thealogy," "the feminist mystic," and "womyn's spirituality." Another term, "womanism," is used by women of color, who in the words of black theologian Delores Williams, "view the world from the underside of history."

I am a profoundly grateful though sometimes uneased observer of the feminist movement, but it goes without question that women are the pacesetters in the creative work of spiritual transformation for a holier globe. We men owe an inestimable debt of thankfulness and appreciation to women for their pioneering work.

Brother-Spirit is being created out of the hearts and minds of men who are unalterably committed to the wisdom of feminist religion. It is created alongside, not in opposition to, womanspirit. We are interested in communion with our sisters. Communion means "building together" and, in parallel fashion, it means nurturing an open and caring conversation between males and females as equals, as religious companions. This communion will require what Shepherd Bliss calls "the de-militarization of language around the genders to refer not to 'the opposite sex' but to 'the other sex' . . . "

Only as we pursue justice and equality for women will our search for intimacy and ultimacy as men be fulfilled. They are intertwined endeavors. Like Siamese twins, they cannot be torn asunder or both will wither.

Given this context there are three fundamental truths which Brother-Spirit espouses.

First, patriarchy is the oldest and most pernicious of injustices. It is degrading to women; it demeans men as well.

> Patriarchy benefits men by giving us a class of people
> (women) to dominate and exploit. Patriarchy also
> oppresses men, by setting us at odds with each other and
> shrinking our life space.[12]

It is a social disease and a spiritual aberration. Brothers reject its motifs of systematic dehumanization. We believe that racism, classism, sexism, ageism, homophobia, military violence, and religious bigotry are offspring of patriarchy and must also be opposed.

Men holding places of power and privilege in American society are the primary perpetrators of physical and psychological violence against other men, themselves, and especially women and children. We men must be brave enough to stand up and speak out, to break the silence and halt the cycle of violence.

We must use our might and our resoluteness to create a world free of violence and overflowing with gender justice and joy. That is our aspiration.

Men must acknowledge our inescapable complicity in patriarchy even as we struggle to destroy it. We are brothers on a new quest to affirm women and men as equal partners in the religious life, *and* we remain patriarchs. We are recovering sexists, yet sexists nonetheless.

John Stoltenberg minces no words in *Refusing To Be a Man:*

> Male supremacy is the honest term for what is sometimes hedgingly called patriarchy. It is the social system of rigid dichotomization by gender through which people born with penises maintain power in the culture over and against the sex caste of people who were born without penises . . .
>
> We have a vision of a world of gender justice, and we want male friends who can enter that world too . . . we want male friends who respect our women friends . . . yet the fact is that each of us is just one man away from selling out our antisexism." [13]

Robert Moore and Douglas Gillette in their trenchant volume, *King, Warrior, Magician, Lover: Rediscovering the Archetypes of the Mature Masculine,* evaluate patriarchy from a different angle:

> In our view, patriarchy is *not* the expression of deep and rooted masculinity, for truly deep and rooted masculinity is *not* abusive. Patriarchy is the expression of the immature masculine. It is the expression of Boy psychology, and, in part, the shadow — or crazy — side of masculinity. It expresses the stunted masculine, fixated at immature levels . . . . Patriarchy is based on fear — the boy's fear, the immature masculine's fear — of women, to be sure, but also fear of men. Boys fear women. They also fear real men. [14]

And near the end of the book they return to the same theme:

> It seems that we as a species live under the curse of
> infantilism — and maybe always have. Thus, patriarchy
> is really "puerarchy" (i.e., the rule of boys).[15]

Such boys oscillate back and forth between the equally damaging conditions of weakness and abusiveness, violence and ineffectiveness. This disparaging yet accurate analysis of modern American men makes even more urgent the work of the Brother-Spirit journey.

The second truth is that authentic brothers are pro-feminist. We applaud and appreciate the life-affirming themes embodied in feminist theology: an earth-centered faith, the interdependent web of all existence, linkage with the cycles and seasons of nature, the belief that everything has consciousness and is sacred, the empowerment of all oppressed people.

If Brother-Spirit resembles these themes, it is because brothers have ignored them at our own peril and our sister's degradation for centuries, and we refuse to do so any longer. These healthy, holy values are to be honored, if at all, in both women and men. It has taken our brave, wise sisters to reawaken the necessity of humanity obeying cosmos-preserving truths.

The third interlocking truth is that, whereas men can support and affirm feminist religion, we cannot fully identify with its source, its power, its cry. Many men become devotees of feminist religion to the extent that they fail to engage their own primary challenges as brothers in today's world. It is misleading, and ultimately counter-productive, for men and women to minimize the distinct edges of our respective agendas.

Men must develop our own religious vision rather than fashion a second-rate version of feminism. Our vision will come from the soil of our male wounds, hungers, and hopes.

Soil or source is the major distinction between Brother-Spirit and feminist theology. We grow our faith-claims from different stories which, in turn, reflect our different physiologies, training, and traits. However, the domain of traits is a fluid category. I agree with Charlene Spretnak's assessment:

> One could simply say that most women naturally possess
> *integrative* skills and most men naturally possess *analytical*

skills. Each person contains both areas in varying
proportions, and both should be developed.[16]

Coming from distinct places of power and privilege, men and
women have theological aspirations that will vary as well. Women
must shed the shackles of subjugation and men, the debilitating
crown of dominance. Women are acknowledging their needs to be
assertive, powerful, and in the foreground. Men are learning how to
be silent, surrendering, and in the background.

Our "homework" assignments — rigorous work at home or
within ourselves — are different. As men search our souls, women
are sharing theirs. We are quieter, they are louder. These revolutions,
inner and outer, are complementary and propel both genders farther
along the road toward development and reconciliation.

Women must deal with mother-daughter, sister, and goddess issues as men confront ourselves in relationship to father, brother, and
god. Let me amplify on the interplay of Brother-Spirit with Father-
God and Mother-Goddess.

Men in Brother-Spirit quest to make peace with Father-God as
well as make room in our religious life for Mother-Goddess. Mature
men covet nourishing bonds with both men and women, Father-God
and Mother-Goddess. Our spiritual diet is imbalanced if we are only
receiving nutriments from one gender or one deity.

Yet our primary male task resides in making sense of and peace
with our oft-fractured relationship with Father-God. Women's as-
signment differs. They have lost their feminine identity through the
ages by being subjugated to a male deity with its attendant patriarchal values and institutions. Women, as feminist theologian Mary
Daly rightly states in her book of the same title, must grow beyond
Father-God and recover Mother-Goddess on the road to healthy
selfhood and sound religion.

There are temptations for each gender. It is tempting for liberated
men to become card-carrying feminists, enamored of goddess wisdom
and imagery, without dealing with the primordial wounds and challenges
for us associated with Yahweh: male creator, destroyer, and sustainer.

Conversely, it is tempting for progressive women to try to "tame"
patriarchal religion, pay continued obeisance to the Judeo-Christian
male God without opening themselves to the primal claims of
Mother-Goddess.

In reading feminist religious literature of recent vintage, I have learned the deficits of patriarchy, the fundamental aspirations of feminist thought, as well as clarified my own Brother-Spirit pilgrimage. I have discovered that Mother-Goddess religion is not for everyone. Numbers of men continue to ignore it and some women downplay its significance. However, I endorse its substance and importance for many reasons.

The first value of goddess religion is historical. As Charlene Spretnak says in the introduction to her book, *The Politics of Women's Spirituality: Essays on the Rise of Spiritual Power Within the Feminist Movement*:

> There is nothing natural about patriarchal religion. It is a relatively recent invention (c. 4500 B.C.). In contrast, artifacts related to the religion of the Goddess are dated as early as 25,000 B.C. [17]

No one — male or female — can be a knowledgeable, responsive religious person without reading about the goddess dimension of religion which has been suppressed and undervalued in Western culture.

A second value of goddess religion emerges as women experience their own stature and identity validated by connecting with a female, elemental power. As Carol Christ writes:

> The simplest and most basic meaning of the symbol of Goddess is the acknowledgment of the legitimacy of female power as a beneficent and independent power. A woman who echoes Ntozake Shange's dramatic statement, "I found God in myself and I loved her fiercely," is saying, "Female power is strong and creative." She is saying that the divine principle, the saving and sustaining power, is in herself, that we will no longer look to men or male figures as saviors. [18]

Men are secondary beneficiaries of the goddess symbol because, in appreciating the earth-centered motifs of goddess religion, we who have been so alienated from the cycles of nature as to dominate and destroy the ecosystem can foreswear our foolish ways and grow a holy alignment with the biosphere.

A third value is that in honoring the goddess we open our lives to a far-ranging cluster of creation spiritualities including Wicca, Native American spirituality, Taoism, Buddhism, Sufism, and Yoga.

It is sometimes easy for men to remain within the cozy confines of the Judeo-Christian faith rather than branch out to explore other religious symbols and practices. Brother-Spirit demands that we grow beyond our provincial thinking as religious searchers.

As David Kinsley states in *The Goddesses' Mirror:*

> The history of religions offers us a rich, diverse and vigorous population of female deities, against which, some might say, the Judaic, Christian, and Muslim pantheons seem one-sided and dull.[19]

A word of caution. Just as it is appealing to characterize all gods as being monochromatic, the same danger lurks with goddesses. Not all goddesses, for example, are linked directly with the Earth and fertility. There is amazing diversity of character. This pluralism of goddesses appeals to those men on the Brother-Spirit quest who covet a plethora of images to flesh out the fullness of divine mystery, remembering that none of our human-fabricated images do justice to the elusive reality of either god or goddess.

Another note of importance. Some goddesses promoted female subjugation to males because they reflected the patriarchal societies in which they thrived. There is ample evidence, however, for goddesses in pre-patriarchal cultures which promoted a greater degree of egalitarianism. Feminist scholars disagree on the strength of the evidence. But these disagreements do not weaken the cause of feminist religion one iota. It is such far-ranging diversity of viewpoint and findings that spawns the kind of tolerance desperately needed in world religions today. As Judith Plaskow and Carol Christ state in the introduction to *Womanspirit Rising:*

> We believe that the diversity within feminist theology and spirituality is its strength. Each of these feminist positions has a contribution to make to the transformation of patriarchal culture. The fundamental commitment that feminists in religion share to end male ascendancy in religion is more important than their differences.[20]

The Horned God is yet a third alternative to the classic Eastern and Western male images of deity as well as a variation of the goddess theme. The Horned God is a bisexual deity espoused by various religionists: Starhawk and Margot Adler, paganists, in their respective volumes, *Dreaming the Dark and Drawing Down the Moon* as well as two male authors, Gary Lingren, who in 1983 started a magazine called "Newsletter of the Brothers of Earth" (later "Brothersong") and John Rowan in his book entitled *The Horned God: Feminism and Men As Wounding and Healing.*

The scholarly research on the Horned God is in its embryonic phase. The champions of the Horned God make this deity into an androgynous blend of female and male qualities.

Listen to Starhawk in *The Spiral Dance:*

> The image of the Horned God in Witchcraft is radically different from any other image of masculinity in our culture. He is difficult to understand, because He does not fit into any of the expected stereotypes, neither those of the "macho" male nor the reverse-images of those who deliberately seek effeminacy. He is gentle, tender, and comforting, but He is also the Hunter. He is the Dying God — but his death is always in the service of the life force. He is untamed sexuality — but sexuality as a deep, holy, connecting power. He is the power of feeling, and the image of what men could be if they were liberated from the constraints of patriarchal culture.[21]

Starhawk goes on:

> The Horned God, however, is born of a Virgin mother. He is a model of male power that is free from father-son rivalry or oedipal conflicts. He has no father; He is his own father. As He grows and passes through his changes on the Wheel, He remains in relationship to the prime nurturing force. His power is drawn directly from the Goddess: He participates in Her.[22]

John Rowan waxes poetic when he says "my spirit rises when I hear Starhawk saying that the Horned God can make men free to be wild without being cruel, angry without being violent, sexual without being coercive, spiritual without being unsexed, and able to truly love."[23]

This portrait of the Horned God is idealistic and appears to promise more than any single god or goddess could deliver us earthlings. What I do find valuable about this male deity and its pagan worshippers is the commitment, as Gary Lingren puts it, to "a positive, non-sexist spirituality from the vantage of changing males committed to the Earth."

I am encouraging men to: 1) confront our unfinished aches and aspirations with Father-God; 2) appreciate and appropriate for our lives wisdom from the goddesses; and 3) pay critical heed to the growing body of literature about the archetypal male deity known as the Horned God.

In closing, a word about Brother-Spirit in the larger context of the contemporary men's movement. Brother-Spirit stands alongside other creative masculine emphases such as Robert Bly's mytho-poetic philosophy, Robert Moore's Jungian analysis, John Rowan's Horned God archetype, and Shepherd Bliss' accent on the Orphic male mysteries of the Mediterranean region. There are other mutually compatible strains of masculine spirituality too.

Men are developing a rich and resourceful interweaving of co-operative, not competitive, spiritual directions for our lives and those brothers who will follow us. We stand together in caring, open dialogue. We all quest for growing intimacy and ultimacy in our lives.

Fellow Travelers

Brothers of Jacob

The bond between Brother-Spirit and feminist theology strengthens as men and women pursue parallel, equally worthy pilgrimages.

Women rooted in feminism and faith have created a journal called *Daughters of Sarah*. It began in 1974 as a women's study and support group seeking to discover what the Bible really says about women. The name "Daughters of Sarah" parallels the Biblical designation "Sons of Abraham."

If I were to launch a new periodical for Brother-Spirit, I would call it "Brothers of Jacob" instead of "Brothers of Abraham." Jacob struggled as son, brother, and father on the agonizing road toward self-fulfillment. Abraham is essentially known, revered, and obeyed in history as a patriarch.

Jacob evolved from the one who seizes from neighbors to the one who strives with God. His transformation presents a viable model for contemporary brothers. His wrestling match is a crossroads experience for all men. When we become our true spiritual selves, we resemble givers not grabbers, honest not deceitful persons, questors not exploiters.

Like Jacob we are never perfect, still weak and wounded, limping yet with a reawakened sense of resolve, powerful from within not over others.

In Jacob, who heals with Esau *and* bonds with God, we have before us a brother moving toward greater intimacy and ultimacy, kinship with the immanent and transcendent presences in existence. Jacob incarnates a synthesis of brothering spirituality. He is a forerunner of the Brother-Spirit quest. Our sage.

We don't adore or worship Jacob. We thank him, applaud and know his struggle as ours, greet him as our brother and invite not his lordship but companionship.

Brothers of Joseph

Another alliance emerges for brothers in the New Testament. Women understandably identify with Mary, Jesus' mother and Joseph's wife. I invite us to consider the underrated yet sound values of Joseph. We have all heard of Mariology. How about Josephology?

Priest Andrew Greeley says that Mary "represents the human instinct that the ultimate is passionately tender, seductively attractive, irresistibly inspiring, and graciously healing." [24]

Women, when they flounder or lose their way, turn to the witness of Mary for guidance, to carry on, to be heartened. Mary does not work as role model or source of strength for all feminists. She reflects the state of subjugation to many. She remains imperfect but helpful to others.

So also Joseph, her oft-forgotten partner. Let's observe the embarrassing yet enlightening context of our father/brother Joseph.

> When his mother Mary had been betrothed to Joseph, before they came together she was found to be with child of the holy spirit, and her husband Joseph, being a just man and not willing to make her a public example, was of a mind to divorce her privately. But as he considered this, behold, an angel of the Lord appeared to him in a dream, saying, "Joseph do not fear to take Mary your wife, for that which is conceived in her is of the holy spirit; she will bear a son and you will call his name Jesus, for he will save his people from their sins." When Joseph awoke, he did as the angel commanded him; he took his wife but knew her not until she had born a son; and he called his name Jesus.
>
> — Matthew 1:18-25

William Willimon amplifies:

> In Galilee, "safe sex" meant an engaged man and woman were not to have intercourse before marriage. If they did, folk in Nazareth called it adultery, no matter what the more sophisticated Jerusalemites called it. Mary was pregnant. Mary's fiancée Joseph was a "just man," a righteous observer of Torah, but not the father of her child. He had two legal options: public divorce with its attendant public humiliation of Mary, in which Joseph's righteous name would be vindicated, or private divorce.

> Mary may have been blessed among women, but
> righteous Joseph was embarrassed among men.[25]

Joseph's behavior provides a powerful lesson for brothers on our sacred journey. The Torah tells Joseph that adultery is adultery. God tells Joseph in a dream to break the law and marry. His conscience breaks the tie; it urges him to act on love not law. He weds Mary and flees to Egypt with his family. Whether his decision was right or wrong, it was his, a decision born of deep reflection and compassion.

Joseph does all this silently. He doesn't deliver a soliloquy or compose a song. He doesn't even speak. He follows the dictates of his conscience, then gets on with life, forgiving Mary and assuming responsibility for the child.

Generous love quietly shared in a scandalous setting.

Joseph is called by my colleague, Bob Schaibly, "the unsung hero of Christmas."

He is more than that. He is our brother, and he was the father of our eldest brother, Jesus. In healing some of the father-son wounds so painful in biblical history and our personal male lives, Joseph presents us with a remarkable example.

One scholar, William E. Phipps, considers the influence of Joseph's loving example upon the moral development of his son, Jesus. He writes:

> Much of a child's theology is communicated to him or
> her by the quality of relationship within the home. Could
> it be that Jesus' rejection of revenge was in part due to the
> influence of Joseph? When Jesus taught "Be merciful,
> even as your father is merciful," could he have had the
> father who reared him in Nazareth in mind? Jesus'
> contemporaries were struck by his audacity in addressing
> God as "Abba," the Aramaic familiar address to Father —
> our equivalent is "Daddy." Jesus' favorite designation for
> God is probably affected by his admiration of the
> character qualities of Joseph.[26]

A footnote about father-love. So much has been written by psychotherapeutic experts in this century, such as Erich Fromm, who downplay "fatherly love as conditional love. I love you *because* you fulfill my expectations . . ." This contrasts with motherly love as unconditional or "I love you as you are." [27]

It's satisfying to have a male/father figure in religious literature like Joseph who embodies accepting, forgiving, and unqualified love. Too often, fathers are unquestioningly stereotyped as second-class parents, second-rate caregivers. Let's hear it for Joseph, the unsung hero of the Christmas story: the exemplary lover, spouse, and father. Our brother.

As we conclude this section, I reiterate that men must be feminists as well as brothers. Indeed I refer to us as feminist brothers. We cannot practice one without pursuing the other. Our imperative is to be pro-brother and pro-sister in balanced fashion. Brothers of Jacob and Joseph honor the daughters of Sarah and Mary as we walk alongside one another. As Rainer Maria Rilke wrote:

> And perhaps the sexes are more related than we think,
> and the great renewal of the world will perhaps consist in
> this, that man and maid, freed from all false feeling and
> aversion, will seek each other not as opposites, but as
> brother and sister, as neighbors, and will come together
> as human beings.[28]

Yet we brothers cannot divest ourselves entirely of our heritage as patriarchs. Jacob couldn't, we can't. We are questors even as we remain oppressors. The highest stature brothers can claim is that of recovering sexists, forgiven oppressors, patriarchs in transition.

We labor unstintingly to do our share in dismantling the dreadful disease of sexual injustice even as we dedicate our existence to the ways of Brother-Spirit. We remain faithful to both pursuits.

Our call for gender justice and reconciliation is our profoundest mission on earth as men and women, as spiritual beings. It lasts our lifetime.

CIRCLES

I have dealt with hurt and hope, alienation and reconciliation among men, especially fathers, sons, and brothers in sample stories from the Bible.

Then I explored the nature of spiritual discipline for contemporary men, recognizing its dangers, benefits, and distinctions. I exhorted us to be full-fledged brothers and feminists in order to create a healthy, holy planet for all creatures.

This section and the next, "Circles" and "Themes," focus on my experience in leading Brother-Spirit workshops and meetings in recent years.

Women have created new rituals, literature, and names. One of the subtle shifts has been to merge words like "womanspirit." I have created a fresh phrase too — Brother-Spirit. I use "brother" to affirm the concerns of intimacy so critical for men today — relationships to self, women, earth, God, and especially other men.

I don't know of a fitting, counterpart word to feminism. I know and respect those who use "masculinism," but it doesn't work for me. "Brother," or "brothering," comes closest because it affirms a relational goal and reality. We are males by birth; we become brothers by choice, deciding to live in healing kinship with the earth and its inhabitants. The concept of "spirit" embodies the concerns of ultimacy which are of highest order in our lives. These concerns will be enumerated in the next section by addressing the religious "themes" of Brother-Spirit meetings.

The hyphen is purposefully used. It provides a bridge between the two precious, powerful pursuits of "brother" and "spirit." It reminds us that both are equally important and inextricably tied together. Sydney Harris, the prominent essayist, confirms my bias:

> Following a college lecture not long ago, somebody in the audience asked me what I thought was the greatest single advance in human knowledge. I replied that it was the use of the hyphen . . . .
>
> The hyphen represents a new way of looking at all life, not in terms of fixed and separate entities, but as interwoven patterns, in a dynamic relationship . . . .
>
> Politics cannot be comprehended without economics and vice versa. Sociology is largely meaningless without psychology. Chemistry and physics are indissolubly linked.[1]

So are Brother *and* Spirit.

RATIONALE FOR MEN-ONLY GROUPS

Men and Women Share Different Stories

Although women have been gathering in women-only or women-identified groups for years, men have only lately been congregating by ourselves — for nurture, conversation, and spiritual support. The simple truth is that both women and men covet separate healing, sharing, celebratory times and spaces. Both genders need sacred circles of their own.

As Alice Walker remarks:

> As a womanist, I am committed to survival and wholeness of entire people, male and female. I am not a separatist, except periodically for health.[2]

Carol Christ makes a similar distinction between separation and separatism for those who fear gender-based circles:

> Separatism as a total world view must be distinguished from instances of separation . . . . Few feminists would deny the validity of women forming groups in which women can share and articulate our spiritual visions with other women. On the other hand, I believe most women in the spirituality movement would be uncomfortable with a *purportedly universal* religion that excluded men or gave only a subordinate role.[3]

One of the richest contributions women and men can make to one another is growing self-differentiation and self-possession, that is, the readiness to befriend the man and woman deep inside ourselves.

We cannot feel or identify directly with the other gender's singular sources of pain, power, and pride. We are inextricably *related to* but not *responsible for* each other's attitudes, behaviors, and journeys.

Men sometimes complain about the need to meet separately: "Why can't we just meet altogether, men and women. After all, isn't human liberation the ultimate goal?" Yes, but there is no easy, short-cut process to reach full liberation. Each gender has specific challenges to address in order to bring more sizeable resources of personhood to our common table.

It is tempting for men to circumvent our gender-based wounds and wishes, and automatically focus on women. It is tempting for men and women to slip into the comfortable old habits of dominance and submissiveness rather than pursue the more rigorous path of colleagueship. It is tempting to engage in courtship ties rather than friendship bonds, born of self-knowledge and mutual respect.

As someone noted: "A whole world needs the fullness of each of us." We women and men labor alone . . . alongside to create a globe of greater gender justice and joy.

Men Are Lone Rangers

Men tend to be lone-ranger types who try to go it alone. Gathering together as men is a stretching, even revolutionary, experience for some of us. We are uninitiated in the craft of collegiality and friendship, so any structured environs to help facilitate deeper bonding is welcome.

A word about the term "meeting." In German there are two words for "meeting": *Sitzung* which means business transactions and *Begegnung* which refers to dialogical encounters. Men have majored in the former kind of meetings and minored in the latter. In our Brother-Spirit meetings we are nudged to face one another in an honest, caring encounter.

My friend Dick has come to the following insight concerning Brother-Spirit meetings:

> God is most present for me as we humans share deep
> dialogue. We brothers travel deeper and deeper until we
> are joined by a presence which transcends us. In that
> sharing, God is present among us.

As Martin Buber, the eminent Jewish theologian, remarked: "All real life is meeting . . . . In each Thou we address the eternal Thou."

And the New Testament reminds brothers that the Kingdom of God (ultimacy) is *entos* — a Greek word meaning both "within" and "among" us — as we gather for moments of brothering (intimacy).

A man pursuing spiritual practice by himself has proven to be a valuable but insufficient process. It is only when the lone rangers band together in tribes that Brother-Spirit comes to fruition. Solitariness must be supplemented with solidarity. Naturally, Brother-Spirit circles are qualitatively distinct from fraternities, sports teams, lodges, military camaraderie, and business partnerships. There is a role for all of those organizations, but they are markedly different in purpose than Brother-Spirit circles.

Alfred North Whitehead in his oft-quoted remark from *Religion in the Making* says: "Religion is what we do with our solitariness." For brothers this means that religion calls us to cherish and enjoy our solitude but not take up residence there.

Authentic religion honors the rhythm of being alone and being together. Whitehead does not say that religion is what we do *in* but what we do *with* our solitariness. This difference has been misunderstood by men who wish to find religious fulfillment solely by themselves.

The word *re-ligare* means literally "to bind together again." Therefore, the full religious adventure calls men to find ourselves, time after time, in fellowship, in circles, in order to incarnate the wisdoms gained in solitude.

Men Need to Care for Each Other

We men need the caring of brothers who face the similar delights and dilemmas of our gender. There are special fears, hopes, expectations which come with the territory of being adult males in today's world.

When you query men, we usually claim to be more at ease with women than men. We have allowed women to be our primary confidantes and companions. This has proven to be a mixed blessing for both genders, often burdensome to women.

As George Lakey, Peter Blood, and Alan Tuttle put it in their evocative pamphlet, "Off Their Backs . . . and On Our Own Two Feet":

> Always going to women for support, play, affection, and care is a key way of oppressing women. Besides, learning how to share these things with men opens up another 50 percent of the human race as potential supporters and personal allies for us! [4]

One of the men in our Brother-Spirit circle grew to this realization:

> My wife pushed me to join our men's support group. She
> thought it would be good for me; I wasn't sure at all.
> Now that I've been on my own with you guys for a few
> months, I know what I've been missing all these years —
> good male friends. My wife's no longer needing to coach
> me, just cheer me on. I'm doing my own dirty-and-
> delight work . . . alongside other men.

There is considerable healing to be achieved between men because we have been pounding upon, even destroying one another, ever since Cain slew his brother Abel. We need to learn respectful, caring ways to be brothers, not to be our brother's boss, keeper, or lackey, but our brother's brother.

Men Need to Confront One Another

Once we spend sufficient time in male-only circles, we grow trust and can risk harsh as well as affirming truths with one another. For as Proverbs 27:6 reminds men: "Faithful are the wounds of a friend."

We can confront each other without being hopelessly combative. For we heed the counsel of our forebrother Hosea Ballou who uttered in 1805: "If we have love, no disagreement can harm us; if we have not love, then no agreement can do us any good."

Where do we occasion or ritualize friendship for men if not in such experiences as Brother-Spirit? Where are men safe enough to *bare* our souls so that someone might *bear* us up if not in the caring, confrontive context of Brother-Spirit?

Dangers Involved in Men-Only Groups

There are dangers to be faced in sharing men-only meetings.

Degenerating into Competitive Clans. We can degenerate into shallow, competitive clans, no different than our traditional ones. We must remember that we are on a quest (journey) — not an inquest (interrogation exercise) or a conquest (victory at all costs).

Our Brother-Spirit philosophy builds collegiality through shared planning, leadership, and programs. We rotate conveners and make decisions by consensus. We work collaboratively, not unilaterally.

Turning Into White, Heterosexual Bastions. Brother-Spirit must intentionally counter the prevailing racist and heterosexist assumptions and practices of society. Inclusivity, while not our accomplishment, remains our constant goal.

Our sacred circles of brothers are partial and incomplete as long as men of color and gay men feel excluded from our fellowship. Brother-Spirit is fueled by the aspiration of becoming a welcoming circle of equal brothers on the quest for growing intimacy and ultimacy.

Becoming Too Dependent on Men-Only Groups. We men can grow addicted to men-identified groups, only feeling safe and secure among members of our own gender. Male-based circles can become male-biased ones if we are not vigilant and balanced.

Brothers need to reaffirm our primary life mission to create gender growth *and* reconciliation. We deepen our own masculine identities as well as build sturdier bridges with women and children.

There is a passage in the Old Testament which I use in keeping men-only meetings balanced efforts to lengthen our companionship as well as strengthen our faith:

> Enlarge the place of your tent, and let the curtains of
> your habitations be stretched out; hold not back,
> lengthen your cords and strengthen your stakes. For you
> will spread abroad to the right and to the left.
>
> — Isaiah 54:2-3

Men need to enlarge the place of our tent. We need to occasion times alone, times with our sisters, times with strangers, times with foes, times with our brothers. We need a wide place in which to grow our brothering.

In strengthening our stakes we plumb the depths of our purpose as men. We sink roots. We furnish anchorage.

In lengthening the cords of our Brother-Spirit quest we reach beyond our own campsite to welcome newcomers, brothers and sisters alike, from the right and the left, from the past, present, and future into our family of soul-companions.

Anchors and expansion, strengthening and lengthening are essentials in our Brother-Spirit adventure.

GUIDELINES FOR BROTHER-SPIRIT CIRCLES

I have found the following guidelines useful in our Brother-Spirit meetings. They keep us comfortable, caring, and on course.

Speak Confessionally

Brothers encourage one another to use "I"-language and speak only for ourselves. We try to make our comments real yet compassionate, "to speak the truth in love," to use the New Testament phrase. We discourage withholders and exhibitionists alike. We try not to resemble Elizabeth Dodson Gray's portrait of the classic male theologian:

> Every time I read male theology I am newly impressed with the pervasive arrogance. There is no existential humility. Men immediately take private, personal ideas coming out of the particularity and specificity of their own lives and experiences (a fact which they conceal from readers), and they make those private, personal reflections into universal truths. I remember reading Paul Tillich's *The Courage to Be* when it was first published. In bringing to bear his great theological and philosophical powers, Tillich never gave any hint of his own personal wrestling with actions or decisions that required of him personal courage.[5]

This confessional demeanor is called the art of "theo-biography" or talking about ultimate things, theological matters, from your heart and personal story.

Build Trust

Speaking *and* listening are married in the climate of trust. As Jacob Trapp mused: "If it is language that makes us human, one half of language is to listen."

Brothers pledge our lives in confidence. We entrust our minds and odysseys into one another's keeping. We handle each other with exceeding care and concern. We receive our brothers' offerings as gifts to enrich our beings, treasures to behold rather than evaluate.

We avoid interrupting or dominating conversation. We refrain from offering unsolicited advice. We promise one another that we will not reveal outside the group what has been daringly ventured inside our circle.

Practice Silence

Too frequently, men hallow only the principle of free speech as we chatter away confidently. The right to reticence is an equally honorable guideline for maximizing our Brother-Spirit sessions. Shy men feel cherished when they know that no brother will pry, weasel, or cajole.

Silence is as venerable a religious practice as dialogue. Silence marks not mere absence of sound but presence of meanings seldom summoned by talkative creatures. In quieting our souls, we withdraw for awhile, then return, refreshed and attentive, ready to give voice to our inner thoughts.

To "contemplate" comes from "*templum,* temple, a space for ob- servation, marked by omens." It means not merely to regard or re- flect, but to do these things in the presence of a god. As the mystics remind us, we need sometimes to travel deeply within, where the divine presence might just be as active as we are.

Foster Community

In everything brothers are and do together we never forget that we are a sacred circle. As minister Shirley Ranck describes:

> Thea-ology of the future must have a new root metaphor —
> a "circle or web of intricate interconnections." [6]

We brothers are building inclusive community where individual men are honored yet transformed and enlarged. Our era covenants like-minded men together in active contemplation and conversation. We dare not risk going it solo anymore. We must be connected. We gather as brothers to foster ongoing community which sustains us while we are together and endures when we are apart.

Grow Rituals

Out of community comes the trust and imagination to grow new, simple, homespun rituals of meaning for the brothers gathered. Here are some examples of ones which our Brother-Spirit meetings have generated over the years.

Common Candle. We begin our Brother-Spirit meetings by lighting our common candle or flaming chalice, either silently or with words like those of brother Oren:

> Now, let us center ourselves in the spirit of consecration and prayer as we light this living flame of our together-ness. May the flame signify for us the Spirit of Life which burns within each of us, a gift which is ours to nurture and to share.[7]

Other times we gather without lighting a candle but focusing on the flame within our hearts. With eyes closed we follow the lead of John Beams:

> Each man can hold hands and picture a warm healing light burning in his center, can envision his heart-river flowing into joined hands and rolling round the circle, can imagine the brilliance in each chest feeding a common fire which grows and touches, enfolds and embraces the whole. Each man can picture spouses, partners, children and pets entering the same circle of light together.[8]

My favorite closing words to which we extinguish our candle are these:

> Knowing how quickly the flame of truth might be extinguished, how easily the chalice of fellowship broken . . . let us be vigilant in faith, keep peace in our hearts and make care for one another. Let us share the watchwords of our lives together so that our light goes out . . . everywhere into the world.[9]

Often our closing words, spoken in unison, are simple ones: "Go gently and safely, back to your homes . . . until we Brother-Spirit again."

Holding Hands. At the end of our Brother-Spirit session we will hold hands in silence, in our sacred circle, with one open spot which symbolizes all those brothers who are absent, ill, on vacation, moved away, disinterested, dead, or scared. We never make a closed circle, because we are never complete. There are always brothers who are not with us on that occasion. We honor them in their absence, we summon them into our presence.

There are moments when we go around the circle mentioning a word or repeating a prayer or mouthing a chant. At times we go around the circle sharing the Hindu blessing, "*namaste*," bowing before each brother with our hands folded in prayer, saying *namaste* which means "may the god in me honor the god in you."

Mid-way Meditation. Sometimes during the course of a heavy, difficult Brother-Spirit meeting, one of us will ask for a respite, some serenity, a change-of-pace — what I call a mid-way meditation. My colleague Vern Curry has just the right kind of spiritual focus to relax our tense group:

> Think of the image of a small stone tossed into a clear pool. Think of yourself as such a stone. Watch it (you) sink effortlessly, floatingly, descending toward the quiet bottom. There it reaches its point of perfect rest. So do you. Watch it sink and settle upon the fine sand of the bottom of the pool. Go there in your imagination and experience that calm. There nothing pushes or pulls as quiet waters flow over and around you. You are at peace in the flow of things. Clarity, calm, and joy attend you in this moment. It is yours. You may return to it, again and again in the days to come.[10]

Then we are called back to the theme of the meeting.

A Mask-uline Exercise. In our Brother-Spirit journey we have spent entire evenings or day-long workshops sharing the ritual of mask-making, then mask-sharing. Men match up in dyads and while evocative, instrumental music fills the room, brothers take turns covering each other's face with vaseline, then wet plaster-of-paris gauze strips, sculpting the mask to the contours of the brother's countenance.

The mask is carefully lifted, dried, painted, followed by intimate dialogue about the experience as well as ceremonial display. Often stories are created and shared in the larger circle, using the masks as catalyzing metaphor. Mask-bearing dances may ensue.

Whenever I have participated in mask-making, I have been startled by the depth of my psycho-spiritual responses. I have experienced ample anxiety and trust in surrendering my face to the sensual caring hands of another man. Reclining on the floor, my sight and voice are gradually shut down and I am quiet, nestled within my interior castle, apart from the familiar world, yet in continuing contact with my brother. Like a good masseur my mask-making partner remains nearby. We are never out-of-touch. For example, even when my companion's hands are briefly away, his knee or foot is touching my body. We are connected from start to finish.

Mask-making is quintessentially a collaborative endeavor. It is my face being shaped, but my brother is the craftsman, and vice versa. The ritual to be whole banks upon utmost cooperation, back and forth, shaper and shaped, active and passive men in caring rhythm.

There are additional anxieties brothers face in this ritual exercise: Will the mask I make resemble my comrade? Will it stick together or collapse? Will he like it? As a male who has felt artistically inept and been labelled so during my formative years, it has been initially intimidating and ultimately liberating to realize that my sacred quest as a man can be explored through my hands as well as my heart and head. Indeed, non-verbal expressions of dance, ritual, and craft are increasingly essential along my brothering path.

The colors I used to paint my first mask were red (my gentle yet fiery warrior side), blue (the mysterious, fathomless sea in which I live, move, and have my being), brown (the deep, lush color of Dean's face, my co-creator), and green (reminder of my vocation to grow eternally).

In a competitive, male-eat-male world, brothers covet safe, trustworthy circles where we can give-and-receive abundantly from one another. Mask-making is a touching ritual of mutual renewal.

Chants. Our Brother-Spirit group employs simple gospel tunes, spirituals like "Kum Bah Yah" or "Peace Like a River," songs which can be easily memorized and recalled. Kent brought to our group a Native-

American chant which has become one of our standards:

> There's a man in me
> There's a man in you
> There's a woman in me
> There's a woman in you
> There's a child in me
> There's a child in you
> There's a god in me
> There's a god in you
> And the man in me loves the man in you
> And the woman in me loves the woman in you
> And the child in me loves the child in you
> And the god in me IS the god in you

> — Words and song from Chief Eagle Feather
> Native American Tribe from the Carolinas

Another prayerful chant which we frequently employ in our Brother-Spirit circles goes as follows:

> I am a circle, I am healing you.
> You are a circle, you are healing me.
> Unite us, make us one.
> Unite us, make us one.

The advantages of a chant are learnability and repetitiveness. It is simple for brothers to anchor in our hearts clear, direct truths via chants.

There are times we neither chant nor sing but hum, melding naturally with one another, as the spirit moves us, without any formal harmony, a rich potpourri of tenor and bass sounds.

Drumming. The Sons of Orpheus, a men's drumming troupe from the Bay Area in California, actually perform in street festivals as well as formal cultural arts gatherings. They are a wonder to behold and hear as *The Berkeley Voice* reports: "Around the dancers were about 20 drum beaters, bell-clangers, and other percussively inclined musicians, all contributing to a mesmerizing African dance beat."

In our renewal weekends or Brother-Spirit evenings back at the ranch, we have a few creative, confident conga drummers who break into our program periodically with their rhythmic, haunting, heart-opening gift. Sometimes we keep going with our conversation or activity; other times we stop and align ourselves with the beat of the drums.

Surrounding the Elders. Our ritual leader, Michael Bauer, created a powerful ceremony involving drums in a recent Brother-Spirit circle of 90 men gathered together in our common lodge.

All men present over sixty years of age were designated as our elders and invited to the center of our large circle. Some twenty men shyly at first, then proudly, stepped forward. Fifteen brothers remained in the circle drumming continuously with a wonderful range of percussion instruments. The remaining brothers were called forth to surround our elders.

Then we were asked to place our right hand upon the shoulder of an elder in front of us and use our left hand to connect with another brother. Slowly we moved to the right, chanting phrases of gratitude and empowerment.

After we completed this spider web ritual of recognition and connectedness, we drummed and danced on into the night. As tears flowed and sweat poured, brothers were bonded and transformed.

Rattle and Sand Dollar. Brother-Spirit member, Michael, has also crafted holy rattles for our group from earthly elements found in our San Diego surrounds. Each one is marked with symbols and colors of poignant meaning for our particular tribe of men. They are replicas of Native American artifacts, which, when shaken, denote our speaking wisdom with power, openness, and love.

Seated around the fire at the Sierra Club Mountain Lodge for our renewals, or sitting in our sacred circles back home, we pass the rattle around and each man, in his own time and manner, shakes it and says: "It is now my turn to speak. I will share my truth among brothers." We don't comment upon the verbal gifts of our soul-kin. We listen with reverence and appreciation.

There are other creations or natural objects which we have used as well in our circles of intimacy and ultimacy. For example, whenever we reveal our grief or wounds, we pass around a sand dollar and utter words like these: "Like this sand dollar, I am both beautifully formed and fragile. I am sturdy *and* vulnerable."

Relic Table. This is simply a table in the middle of our sacred circle which is adorned, from time to time, with personal treasures brought to it by our brothers. These are ordinary yet precious relics which signify a moment of pain, a memory of joy, or a life-transition. They reside there as silent artifacts or are described by the brother who gifted us with it. It is our memorabilia table — graced with pictures, rocks, creations, mystery items. Holy objects, one and all.

Male Initiation Ceremony. Brother-Spirit has been interested in creating appropriate rites of passage for the younger boys in our religious family, especially the teenagers. We are working on such ceremonial transitions, but a first priority has been to fashion our own adult male rite wherein we would be welcomed into "the circle of men." Few men could remember a significant initiation ritual during their formative years. Now was the time for our Brother-Spirit community to occasion a rite of passage.

Brother Michael accomplished this with the simple yet powerful ceremony which follows:

> I am Raven, and I have been sent here by Father Sky to host this ceremony of transition in the Circle of Men. I am here because I am the bringer of magic and because Father Sky wanted me to call upon the medicine of Brother Snake and Brother Wolf. With me here tonight are representatives from the four directions.
>
> I have hosted many of these ceremonies, and all of them have two things in common: something is left behind, and something emerges and carries on. Usually there is a point in the ceremony where a transition or transformation takes place. The child is left behind, and the man emerges. This transformation is experienced through a catalytic confrontation. Sometimes I ask the individual to face a wild animal and risk possible injury. Sometimes I ask the individual to face an enemy and risk possible death. Tonight I offer you the ultimate confrontation as a male: I ask you to face yourself and risk possible life.
>
> To begin tonight, the rattle of truth will be passed around. You may choose to speak or be silent, for there is some-times more truth in silence. If you choose silence, pass on the rattle. If you choose to speak, shake the rattle, leave it on your chair, and take your stick to the hearth. State your name, break the stick, and tell the Circle what it is that you leave behind. Then, throw half of your stick in the fire. The medicine of Brother Snake will be honored when the Circle of Men responds with your name and, "We celebrate your shedding of skins." Next, tell the Circle what it is that

you bring with you and throw the other half of your stick in the basket that represents the gifts to the Circle of Men. The medicine of Brother Wolf will be honored when the Circle of Men responds with your name and, "We celebrate your gift."

When all have spoken who choose to do so, the basket of gifts to the Circle of Men will be purified in the flames.

After the men shared from their hearts and histories, our male initiation ceremony closed with the following responsive reading:

East	As individuals, we have shed the unwanted aspects of the past, and have celebrated their transformation by fire.
South	As the Circle of men, we have joined together our unique gifts of the present and future, and we have celebrated their purification by fire.
West	We have chosen what to leave behind, and what to bring with us. We have shared these choices with the Circle of Men.
North	Our ability to choose and to live with the consequences, positive or negative, is the sign of our transformation from child to man.
Sky (Raven)	And so it is that if we leave behind the fears of the child and bring with us a commitment to the development of our self-esteem,
Earth	. . . We are welcomed into the Circle of Men.
Sky	If we leave behind the naiveté of the child and bring with us a commitment to the development of our clarity and strengths,
Earth	. . . We are welcomed into the Circle of Men.
Sky	If we leave behind the innocence of the child and bring with us a commitment to the development of our male sexuality,
Earth	. . . We are welcomed into the Circle of Men.
Sky	If we leave behind the material concerns of the child and bring with us a commitment to the development of our spiritual concerns,

Earth	. . . We are welcomed into the Circle of Men.
Unison	Sometimes the child asks the man a question. He expects an answer based on wisdom and experience. As we move into the circle of men, may we not forget, when in need, to ask the child within for an answer based on innocence and wonder.

Two closing thoughts. First, the richest rituals are those which are homegrown, so be attentive in your Brother-Spirit explorations to creative possibilities.

Second, our rituals should be fun rather than somber. We men rarely act silly or allow our child out into the open. Brother-Spirit rituals encourage playfulness. In describing the rituals of Witchcraft, Starhawk offers words applicable to our Brother-Spirit rites:

> Rituals are active, physical, energetic, and cathartic. Ecstasy and wild, untamed energy are given a spiritual value, not relegated to the football field or the corner bar.[11]

Live the Questions

> I want to beg you as much as I can . . . to be patient
> toward all that is unsolved in your heart and to try to love
> the questions themselves. . . . Live the questions now.
> Perhaps you will then gradually, without noticing it, live
> along some distant day into the answer . . . [12]
>
> — Rainer Maria Rilke

The most important guideline in Brother-Spirit meetings might be the question approach. Our times together are launched and sustained by questions to which we give heartfelt, honest responses.

Why are questions so important to men?

Questions, more than direct counsel or fervent exhortation, evoke our depths, expand our horizons, and nourish the growth of our souls.

We men are so busy and preoccupied in our daily lives that we fail to stop and take stock of our existence. We are too rushed to even raise questions: Who are we? Where are we headed? Why are we placed on earth? How can we serve the Creation?

Perhaps these basic questions terrify us. Perhaps we are nervous about the responses we might make.

The questions we are more likely to raise on any given day are ones like: What happened on the stock market today? Did the NFL strike end? Gretchen, do you have any money for your lunch at school? Who will baby-sit, dear, for the kids when we have our dinner engagement on Friday night?

There's nothing wrong with mundane, daily questions like these. We all ask them. We all answer them. We have to in order to survive. However, the point of human existence is not mere survival but life — abundant, satisfying life.

And the best way for men to move towards a fulfilling life is to raise the profounder questions and wrestle mightily with them, day and night.

I have always been fascinated by the fact that one of the first things out of God's mouth in the Old Testament was a probing question to Adam and Eve: "Where are you?" (Genesis 3:9) which was not merely a question of geography but morality and relationship as well. Where are you in relationship to your purpose on earth, where are you in relationship to your partner, where are you in relationship to your Creator? Men spend the rest of our lives trying to mount creative answers to these queries. We don't solve them on the spot or overnight. Our very lives are our most revealing response.

Questions are also a gentle, open-ended way for us to deal with challenges of being fulfilled men. Questions invite us, at our own pace, to respond in our own way. They evoke, maybe even provoke, without pressuring us.

Men have traditionally been answer-givers. We feel secure in answers. We make points and strides in life with our answer-giving experience and agility. We have answers sometimes even before questions are asked.

Yet as questors for intimacy and ultimacy, brothers must become eminent question-raisers, even when no adequate responses are forthcoming. Sam Keen puts it strongly:

> To be on a quest is nothing more or less than to become
> an asker of questions. In the Grail legend, the classical
> tale of male heroism, we are told that when the Knights
> of the Round Table set out on their quest, each one
> entered the forest at the place it was darkest and forged a

path where none had been before. The inner, psychological meaning of this myth is that full manhood is to be found only when we commit ourselves to a life of questioning.[13]

The following questions are ones which have grown out of my own Brother-Spirit quest, my own growing struggle with self, neighbor, nature, and God. They are the ones which haunt me, popping up in the middle of the night, or during a meditative moment at work or play.

Some are aspirational and have pushed and pulled me. Others are abrasive and persistent and have nagged away at my spirit despite repeated attempts to put them to rest.

However, these questions don't only belong to me. They aren't original. They have been asked at one time or another throughout human history. I have read them in one version or another. I have heard them in different forms in my counseling and conversation with countless male compatriots, from nearly twenty years of leading and participating in the men's movement, and from Brother-Spirit workshops and retreats.

Remember there is no one right answer to any of the spirit-stretching questions which ensue. There are my answerings plus yours, but no definitive answers.

Composer John Cage once said: "That is a very good question. I should not want to spoil it with an answer." Sometimes these questions themselves will prove sufficient. They won't require an answer, only our creative mulling.

Good questions don't bring easy resolution; they push us to new heights of understanding and awe. Good questions breed more questions, so be prepared to generate queries of your own even as you dance with mine.

Thomas Merton, one of the spiritual giants of the twentieth century, said that "we are known better by our questions than by our answers." Keep that in mind.

THEMES

The typical format for a Brother-Spirit circle includes:

— centering ritual or song;

— a community check-in where we share what's current in our hearts; and

— the thematic focus of the session which is explored via questions.

There is time for each brother to reflect upon and respond to the question by himself, then opportunity to share in dyadic dialogue with another brother, and finally time for group conversation in response to the questions for the meeting.

Our evenings close with a prayer or a chant in the sacred circle. The themes for our Brother-Spirit sessions have been:

1) Re-Membering Our Past

2) Fulfilling Our Selves

3) Loving Our Neighbors

4) Pursuing Truths

5) Engaging Our Brothers

6) Making Peace With the Earth

7) Honoring Our God

8) Becoming Good Fathers and Good Sons

RE-MEMBERING OUR PAST

I am stirred by the thought of the number of people
whom I have to thank for what they gave me or what
they were to me.[1]

— Albert Schweitzer

There is no standing still in life; we are either forging ahead or coasting downhill. One of the basic ways brothers grow is by paying homage to our pasts. We make peace with the events and people who have gone before us, influencing our existence.

If we don't "re-member," that is, bring beings and realities back into our memory and current membership, we essentially dis-member them. Our lives unravel and scatter.

We have spent an entire Brother-Spirit meeting going around the circle with each man calling to consciousness the irrepeatable significance of males in our lives: friends, fathers, sons, uncles, brothers, cousins, foes, associates, lovers, etc. The memories can be pleasant, sad, ambivalent. The tears flow, particularly when saluting those of blessed memory. The haunting refrain, "I still miss him," echoes through the room. We keep going around the circle until everyone runs out of remembrances.

The instructions can be more specific for a given session. We can focus upon the men in our family, those we haven't seen since boyhood, those with whom we have unfinished business, or those men whom we haven't thanked. We bring them back, greet them in spirit, then let them travel on in our memory. After each man is remembered, the group might say together, "Three cheers for Ralph" or "Ralph, we remember and celebrate you," speaking the name of the recalled person.

This activity proves a powerful, intergenerational one for men and boys, because everyone has memories to share. It bridges and bonds men of all ages.

The value of re-membering people from our past is demonstrated in Charles Kuralt's conversation with Lowell Davis:

> On the road in Savannah, Missouri, I stopped by Lowell Davis's house, because I'd heard he'd written a book.
>
> Of course, nowadays everybody seems to have written a book . . . a diet book, cat book, or how-to-get-rich book. Lowell Davis never knew how to get rich. He had a hard life as a farmer and sign painter and small storekeeper. But he met a lot of people, and that's what his book is about.
>
> His book is simply a list of everyone he has ever met, every single person he can remember. That's eighty-four years of remembering.
>
> Kuralt: How many names do you have in there now?
>
> Davis: I believe I got 3584.
>
> Kuralt: Have you met some whose names you don't care to remember?
>
> Davis: Yes, I do sometimes . . . but I put 'em down anyway.
>
> The names are arranged in chronological order, grouped by all the different towns he has lived in. Sometimes he can't remember a name. But then, sometimes his wife, Hazel, can. They've been married fifty-seven years, so they've met a lot of the same people.
>
> The book begins where it ought to. At the beginning.
>
> One of Lowell Davis's neighbors, when he heard about the book, said, "Well, I suppose there are worse ways of wasting your time." But of course, it is not a waste of time. It is one man's way of summing up his life. In doing so, Lowell Davis has conferred a little bit of immortality on every man and woman who has come his way.[2]

Here are some questions I have invited brothers to consider during this "Re-Membering Our Past" session.

I. Create a religious life-line depicting your spiritual odyssey, re-membering persons, moments, institutions from birth until now.

What naming ceremony, if any, marked your birth as a baby?

Did you have "religious" experiences during your growing-up years? Experiences by yourself, with nature, in the presence of God? In a fellowship setting?

What have been the "crises," the turning points, in your religious maturing?

Reflect upon births and deaths of friends and loved ones during your life. What influence did they have upon your spiritual growth?

II. Religion has often been described as a growth-producing mix of joys and sorrows. Re-membering specific joys and sorrows, how have you expanded your existence because of them?

We men are hard pressed to reveal our losses and our failures in most groups, but when we are surrounded by an affirming, supportive Brother-Spirit group, we open up and grow up.

Our forebrother, Theodore Parker, wrote in the nineteenth century that there was no sorrow which he could afford to lose. All of them helped to enlarge his humanity.

III. The Ten Commandments in our lives

I have spent two or three sessions simply on the Ten Commandments. The first evening we determine the relevance of each recommendation for our lives from this venerable decalogue in the book of Exodus. The next meeting we study other versions of the Ten Commandments composed by prominent historical figures.

The final gathering centers on each man crafting his own original list, however long or short, of principles by which he lives. We don't put pressure on one another; some brothers come up with but a few governing values while others generate a veritable laundry list. I remind my companions that Woody Allen announced that "ten suggestions" might be the best we moderns could produce.

A fruitful meeting can be similarly spent with the beatitudes in the New Testament. The imaginative, poetic phrasing men allow ourselves in these exercises is exhilarating to behold. The process is as crucial as the product.

IV. Looking back, what have been your most gratifying achievements thus far? Your most discouraging shortfalls?

One of our male proclivities is to evaluate our stories in terms of *doing*. The more we brothers trust one another, the more our stories disclose our very *being*. An example was Samuel who early on in our group declared his accomplishments in terms of athletic statistics and business deals. As time passed and as trust grew, he began to reveal his inner aspirations to be a loving father, a steadfast husband, a faithful son, and a thankful child of the universe. But it took time and trust.

V. Events shape our religious faith. What are the two or three formative events in your life? Why are they memorable to you?

Alex told us a painful, pivotal event in his life. "When I shit in my pants in kindergarten, I was mocked by the other kids, scolded by the teacher. Then I went home emotionally bruised and forlorn to my mother. Much to my surprise and enormous relief, Mom welcomed me, helped me clean up, brought me fresh clothes, and took me out to the park to play with her.

"I have never forgotten how my ugly, hurt self was transformed by my mother's gestures of love. I felt unconditionally accepted by her. I return to that event whenever I doubt my self-worth."

One of the pivotal moments in my own life occurred when I went home to my parents after my first wife and I separated. Guilty, weeping, unsure of what to expect, I was greeted by my Dad who said: "Tom, I don't like what has happened, but I don't care why you did it. You are our son. You will always be welcome here. Your old room is yours!"

My buddy George unequivocally designated his birth as the fundamental event in his spiritual odyssey. His mother had had five miscarriages previous to his birth. He was truly a miracle. His mother felt so and always reminded him of his miraculous nature, a reminder which has proved to be both a blessing and burden in his life.

Our experiences don't have to be conventionally or institutionally "religious" to be sacred passages.

FULFILLING OUR SELVES

> What is my place in the middle of this chaotic and noisy world? [3]

> — Thomas Merton

Brother-Spirit contends that mature men are able to balance the four primary loves of our existence: love of self, neighbor, nature, and God. Our lives are spiritually askew or lopsided if we stay impoverished in any of these four areas.

The cornerstone is a healthy dose of self-love, not self-infatuation but bedrock appreciation of and affection for our unique, irrepeatable presences on earth.

Men and women generally have different struggles with self-esteem. Women are acculturated to have underdeveloped self-concern. Men end up with inflated egos. Each gender has homework to redress the imbalance. Our spiritual stock-taking begins with self.

I. Who am I?

Write simple notes or a prose-poem to capture the current relationship to your body, mind, heart, conscience, spirit.

What follows is a love letter to myself composed years back. As every brother knows, the responses to this question will vary, almost weekly, depending upon current self-appraisal.

Dear Me,

I think you already know and feel it, me, but I'm very fond of you. It's important that I say that out loud, now, for all to hear, because that hasn't always been the case.

In the early going I was mighty hard on you. I would put you down before I would raise you up. I was much tougher on you than others were!

Now, I have an abiding fondness for you despite your fumbles and foibles, your outbursts of ugliness, your lousy habits. In spite of all your shortcomings, I love you, me. Can you feel my love? Can you receive it?

How do I love you, me? Let me count the ways.

I am grateful for your heart. It does what a heart is made for — it pumps caring most of the time.

I enjoy your body. You're taking better care of it now than ever before. It shows it. Keep nourishing your body all the way home. Even learn to caress your wrinkles, my friend. And don't turn to Grecian Formula: I like your salt-and-pepper look. Don't mess with your aging processes.

I appreciate your mind. It's limited, for sure, but you use a whole lot of what you've got. You have been known to be wise upon occasion. I like your spirit. It stays in motion, open, alert, and can soar. Keep it fit.

In closing, my buddy, I offer a few tough encouragements:

-   lighten up, laugh more deep, belly laughs

-   sing as much as you can, for singing opens up your deepest regions

-   let some things in your life fade away and practice dispensability

-   be quiet, be still, be . . .

Love,

Your Buddy,

I

II. What do you like to do when no one else is around?
This is a playful, spirit-expanding exercise.

III. When are you enthusiastic (literally, "god-filled") in your life?

Men are often surprised by our reflective discoveries in response to this question.

IV. What are the demons or fears blocking you from your calling, your enthusiasm, your fulfillment?

For all the talk about men being macho and brave, the most common demon possessing males is cowardice. It rears its ugly head in many forms:

— "I want to have a permanent, satisfying partnership, but I'm scared to commit myself."
— "I am unwilling to make the economic and social sacrifices necessary to sustain racial equality."
— "I am frightened by too much closeness with men."
— "I can't easily admit my weaknesses to my kids."
— "I don't want to die."

Jesus urged us to pay homage to "the enemies within our own household." Another male proclivity is to project onto outside forces or people — usually women and children — our inner demons, which need to be faced, made truce with, and whenever possible, ousted.

Who are the dark, shadowy demons within your lives and can you *brother* them?

The enemies and friends within our own household are often amazingly akin. As Henri Nouwen writes:

> It indeed is not so strange that sentimentality and cruelty
> are found in the same people. The image of Hitler,
> moved to tears by a small child, stands in the memory of
> many who witnessed his merciless cruelties.[4]

So also with you and me.

Walt Whitman asked: "Do I contradict myself? Yes, for I contain multitudes." Men are tormented creatures, trying to juggle paradoxes inside our hearts and minds. Sometimes we remain relatively intact with our internal tensions. Other times the inner strife is so fierce, we need healing.

There is a relevant Hasidic tale:

> The son of a Rabbi went to worship on the Sabbath in a
> nearby town. On his return, his family asked, "Well, did
> they do anything different from what we do here?" "Yes,
> of course," said the son. "Then what was the lesson?"
> "Love thy enemy as thyself." "So, it's the same as we say.
> And how is it you learned something else?" "They taught
> me to love the enemy within myself." [5]

Russian novelist, Fyodor Dostoevsky, was not only a literary genius but also something of a sacred psychologist. In his greatest novel,
The Brothers Karamazov, he dealt with unifying our torn personali-
ties. In the preface, Andrew H. MacAndrew states:

> In the fate of the brothers Karamazov each of us recog-
> nizes his own fate. The writer portrays the three brothers
> as a spiritual unity. This is an organically collective
> personality in its triple structure: the principle of reason is
> embodied in Ivan: he is a logician and rationalist, an
> innate skeptic and negator; the principle of feeling is
> represented by Dmitry: in him is the "sensuality of
> insects" and the inspiration of eros; the principle of will,
> realizing itself in active love as an ideal, is presented in
> Alyosha.
>
> The main hero of Karamazov is the three brothers in
> their spiritual unity. Three personal themes are developed
> parallel, but on the spiritual plane the three parallel lines
> converge: the brothers, each in his own way, experience a
> single tragedy, they share a common guilt and a common
> redemption. [6]

V. What must you be or do to be "saved"?

I read somewhere the story of a plain-dressed Dunkard accosted
on the street of a town in Pennsylvania by an eager, evangelical young
man who asked, "Brother, are you saved?" The long-bearded Dunkard
did not respond immediately. He pulled out a piece of paper and
wrote on it, then handed it to the stranger. "Here," he said, "are the
names and addresses of my family, neighbors, and people with whom
I do business and play. Ask these people if they think I am saved.
Why, I could tell you anything."

That's the way it was with my father too, as well as with many other men we could name. My Dad never was a churchgoer. He never talked about salvation, his or anyone else's. But if asked if he were saved, he would have probably passed on a list of references. After all, isn't that the only way to test one's salvation — to take a long look at our track record as noted by our companions and acquaintances along life's road?

LOVING OUR NEIGHBOR

Who is my neighbor? Everyone, especially those in need, replies the New Testament. And how much should I love my neighbor? The answer: as much as — neither more nor less than — myself.

This Brother-Spirit theme focuses on respecting, appreciating, reconciling with, and loving our neighbors: the men, women and children who people our lives.

I am reminded of two passages in the New Testament:

> So if you are offering your gift at the altar, and there re-
> member that your brother has something against you,
> leave your gift there before the altar and go; first be recon-
> ciled to your brother, and then come and offer your gift.

> — Matthew 5:23-24

I start this session by letting my brothers know that talking and praying about neighbor-love is never as important as actually making peace with him or her. So, if they choose, they may leave a gift at the altar, then be excused to go forth and reconcile with someone who holds a grudge against them.

The second New Testament passage is self-evident:

> If anyone says, "I love God," and hates his brother, he is
> a liar; for he who does not love his brother whom he has
> seen, cannot love God whom he has not seen.

> — I John 4:20

Using "male" language makes this truth even more impressive.

Both of these passages are sobering reminders for brothers as we launch our sacred quest to love our neighbor.

I. What are three relationships where you need to give and/or receive forgiveness?

Since forgiveness is the highest form of love, brothers need to grapple with its implications early on in any meaningful dialogue on neighbor-love.

For most men, the heaviest, most anguishing alienation is with parents and/or children, whether we live with them or not. There are unspeakable wrongs to be righted and breaks to be healed in our realities as sons and fathers.

II. Where are you growing in relation to "minorities": persons of color, the physically handicapped, the mentally retarded or emotionally disturbed, the homeless, seniors, and gays and lesbians?

Most brothers I know are struggling valiantly to move from fear to trust, disdain to acceptance with respect to all so-called "minorities." It is an uphill struggle.

III. When is your display of anger charitable and productive rather than destructive?

Most brothers know how to fight, but we don't always fight fairly and constructively. We may fight passively or with vengeance. We need to learn ways to be *positively* angry, to channel our male frustrations toward impact rather than injury.

Jack has three strategies he uses: "I fight best when I don't take things personally, when I quit trying to change the other person, and when I want resolution more than to be right."

I think the most important insight in dealing with our anger is for men to realize that intimates stay close and share anger rather than flee. In his book entitled *A Man and His God,* Martin Pable, priest and psychologist, states:

> Even Moses, whom the Bible calls God's "intimate friend" (Ex. 33:12), got exasperated with God on more than one occasion and told him so. One time, when the Israelites were getting tired of their daily ration of manna and wanted some good meat for a change, Moses lost his cool and had it out with the Lord:

"Why do you treat your servant so badly?" Moses asked the Lord. "Why are you so displeased with me that you burden me with all these people? Was it I who conceived them, or was it I who gave them birth . . . ? Where can I get meat to give to all this people? . . . I cannot carry all of them by myself, for they are too heavy for me. If this is the way you will deal with me, then please do me the favor of killing me at once, so that I need no longer face this distress" (Nm. 11:11-15).[7]

Give examples of where you are robustly and resolutely angry for change in your life.

IV. Where are your comfort *and* discomfort zones with women?

When do you feel engulfed by and when embraced by women? What has to happen to enable you to call a woman your sister?

PURSUING TRUTHS

Truth comes to earth in small installments.

— Clinton Lee Scott

I. Partial Truth or Whole Truth?

A colleague once told me, "What you are saying, Tom, may just well be a 100-percent half-truth." So often that's the case, isn't it? We men race off, feeling content, even smug, about our hard-earned insight, only to learn that there are many genuine views on that issue and what we are fiercely clutching as ultimate is but a partial truth. We have fallen desperately in love with a toe, an earlobe, or an elbow. We are captivated with parts rather than being open to the whole experience, the whole person, the whole truth.

Truth not only comes in small installments but is often downright confusing. Some years ago I saw a cartoon in the *New Yorker* created around the idea that if you could sit monkeys in front of typewriters and let them type long enough, eventually, just by chance, one of them would type out the whole Bible, or the complete works of Shakespeare.

In the *New Yorker* there was depicted this monkey, seated in front of a typewriter, clicking away; and what you read over the monkey's shoulder on the typewriter paper is: "To be or not to be, that is the Gazorninplotz!"

Our trek toward wisdom may seem flawless. Everything is perfectly set up, and whoops, we end up with part insight and part obfuscation, just like the monkeys. We are poised to grasp the truth, and then we produce our own "Gazorninplotz"!

We forget that pursuit of the whole truth is a tricky, twisting, endeavor not meant for brittle hearts or flabby souls.

We brothers must remember that truth comes in small installments, that our truths are partial, that our truths end up a crazy mix of enlightenment and nonsense. There is no shame in admitting our mistakes or changing gears in midstream, either.

Mahatma Gandhi once led a protest march in which many thousands of people left their jobs and homes to endure great hardship. As the march was well underway, Gandhi called a halt and disbanded it. His lieutenants came to him and said, "Mahatma, you can't do this; the march has been planned for a long time and there are so many people involved." Gandhi's simple answer was, "My friends, my commitment is to truth as I see it each day, not to consistency."

Men on the Brother-Spirit quest are committed not to the closed mind nor the empty mind but to the open mind that follows the fresh insights and intuitions of each new day.

What are the primary truths which drive your spiritual existence? List five and then describe the ways in which these installments have come into your life?

II. Prejudice

Men must be aware of confusing our private habits with larger truths, our prejudices with wisdom. Anthony De Mello tells the story of the guru's cat. When the guru sat down to worship each evening the ashram cat would get in the way and distract the worshipers. So he ordered that the cat be tied during evening worship. After the guru died the cat continued to be tied during evening worship. And when the cat expired another cat was brought to the ashram so that it could be duly tied during evening worship. Centuries later learned treatises were written by the guru's scholarly disciples on the liturgical significance of "tying up a cat while worship is performed."

That's a gruesome story, but it remains all too true in the history of our practices as men. Frequently, we confuse our long-standing conventions with eternal truths. Basing our lives on unexamined assumptions, we tie up cats, not to mention people on stakes.

To discover truths, we must be willing to sweep prejudice and superstitions aside.

Which of your beliefs might be harboring biases or prejudices?

Which of your convictions resemble gambles and which ones seem secure?

III. Seek, Find, and Tell the Truth

Being a truth-seeker isn't sufficient for men pursuing the Brother-Spirit path. There is nothing wrong with our desire to be truth-seekers as long as we don't halt with the search, as long as we don't make a terminal value out of an instrumental one.

The painter Pablo Picasso, certainly an open-minded person, decries the idolatry of searching endlessly without discovery when he wrote:

> In my opinion, to search means nothing in painting. To find, is the thing. The one who finds something, no matter what it might be, at least arouses our curiosity, if not our imagination. When I paint, my object is to show what I have found and not what I am looking for.[8]

Those of us engaged in Brother-Spirit are seekers and finders, both. Even though our findings are never final, they furnish operating wisdoms to guide our lives.

Having found some truth, we are then challenged to face the consequences of what we've found. Truth-facing is frequently disturbing and painful, at times socially unpopular, and occasionally downright dangerous. As Flannery O'Connor quipped: "Find the truth and it shall make you odd."

There are truths we men would rather ignore: truths about ourselves, about our jobs, about our inherited beliefs, about our parents or children, about our friends or lovers, about our country, about our chosen ideologies.

I ask men: "What are some of the surprise truths you've discovered? What are some of the painful, awkward ones?"

Once brothers have *found* some truth, then we need to *tell* our truth. Speaking truth in a world where truth-telling isn't particularly valued, either privately or publicly, is no easy challenge.

Most men can share truisms, platitudes, Hallmark card sentiments, but the deeper, abrasive, dangerous truths confound us. Telling the truth is much more complex and difficult than either telling lies or keeping silent.

Can you tell your brothers about times in your life when you have spoken the truth? When you have, for better or worse, withheld truth? When would you tell lies?

IV. Doing the Truth

Finally, after we seek, find, and tell truths, then we must *do* the truth. Embodying truths in our daily life is the litmus test of the authentic brother. As Buckminster Fuller said, "Truth is a verb . . . " and the New Testament exhorts us, above all else, "to do the truth" not just chat about it, pay homage to it, or toy with it.

We think about the inspiration of Albert Schweitzer who wrote: "My life . . . my argument!" At the age of thirty, he stood at the peak of his promise as theologian, Biblical scholar, organist, foremost interpreter of Bach, and professor. He gave it all up to serve the Africans in one of the most disadvantaged areas of the world at that time.

He built a hospital with his own two hands. He raised both money and a staff. When once he asked a local friend, who was well educated, to help him carry some heavy timber, the answer was, "I am an intellectual, and don't carry timbers around," to which Schweitzer replied, "You're lucky. I too wanted to become an intellectual. But I didn't make it."

We brothers belong to an intelligent group but we are not a band of intellectuals. We are called to be truth-doers, carrying around the necessary timbers to build a just and merciful society.

We close this Brother-Spirit circle by reviewing our truth-doing experiences as men. When have you been a sage, willing to incarnate your wisdom?

Name three times when your soul has been on fire and your life an "argument" for justice and compassion.

ENGAGING OUR BROTHERS

> I know that the spirit of God is the brother of my own,
> And that all the men ever born are also my brothers . . .
>
> — Walt Whitman
> from *Song of Myself*

There will always be brothers of the road and brothers of the spirit: the former whom you befriend in unlikely places or under intense circumstances and whom you may never meet again and the latter with whom you have abundant time to explore and expand your bond. As George Santayana remarked: "We all have friends in pieces." Men tend to burden one or two relationships with unfair expectations. Or we compare and rank friends — an odious practice.

We are in better brothering shape when we admit having brothers in parts. I play tennis with my buddy Pete. I have regular lunch with my friend John. With Jeremy we swap our hurts and help one another through them. We are our own version of the "Bruise-Blues Brothers." I have heart talk with a half-dozen men from time to time.

These are all meaningful brothers in my life. In our ongoing Brother-Spirit sessions, we are able to develop some length and depth in our bonds, although we may be selective in following-up on certain ties. Some of us are friends primarily in the Brother-Spirit group; we desire little contact outside.

In short, men are brothers in pieces, never complete, closer and dearer with some than others. We must learn to accept this reality.

A powerful, life-affirming account of brothering is found in *No Laughing Matter,* written by Joseph Heller and his best friend Speed Vogel. It is an unusual book which salutes the friendship in Joseph Heller's life with Mario Puzo, Mel Brooks, Dustin Hoffman, and especially Vogel. Here is a relevant excerpt on friendship:

> Dustin and I had become acquainted about ten years
> earlier and we would get together for dinner or lunch

from time to time if we chanced to meet in the same city. A reason we have remained such good friends is that we have never been close ones. We have never worked together, and that too has undoubtedly helped, leaving each of us with an unmarred respect for the judgment and consideration of the other that is probably unwarranted by both. Between us as the foundation for our friendship are the ground rules I promulgated once only partly in jest: he doesn't have to read my novels, and I don't have to see his movies.[9]

A fine friendship from Eastern scriptures is found in the Gilgamesh Epic which begins with a wrestling match between Gilgamesh and Enkidu that ties together all the episodes in the story. It is reminiscent of Jacob's wrestling match.

> Mighty Gilgamesh came on and Enkidu met him at the gate. He put out his foot and prevented Gilgamesh from entering the house, so they grappled, holding each other like bulls. They broke the doorposts and the walls shook, they snorted like bulls locked together. They shattered the doorposts and the walls shook. Gilgamesh bent his knee with his foot planted on the ground and with a turn Enkidu was thrown. Then immediately his fury died. When Enkidu was thrown he said to Gilgamesh, "There is not another like you in the world. Ninsum, who is as strong as a wild ox in the byre, she was the mother who bore you, and now you are raised above all men, and Enhil has given you the kingship, for your strength surpasses the strength of men." So Enkidu and Gilgamesh embraced and their friendship was sealed.[10]

Physical contact, whether friendly or confrontive, is a vital element in the development of male-male friendships.

The genius and strength of brothering is equality. To be friends men must treat one another as peers. It is hard for men in a counseling situation, employer-employee context, or even the father-son dynamic to be bona fide friends, because in all these relationships we are enmeshed in an hierarchical exchange, however modified.

Take, for example, Sigmund Freud and Carl Jung, giants of psychoanalysis who were mentor and disciple to each other. Their friendship couldn't transcend this gulf. As Perry Garfinkel recounts:

> In the early years of their relationship Jung continued to

put Freud on the hero's pedestal. "My veneration for you has something on the character of a 'religious crush.'" Ironically, the issue of religion and its place in analysis would eventually cause their schism.

At one point in their correspondence, Jung suggested a form by which they continue their interpersonal liaison: "Let me enjoy your friendship not as one between equals but as that of father and son. This distance appears to me fitting and natural. It strikes a note that would prevent misunderstanding and enable two hard-headed people to exist, alongside one another in an easy unrestrained relationship." [11]

Freud had his difficulties with a relationship of equals too. Ernest Jones reports that "Freud felt guilty all his life because of his death wishes, based on jealousy, which he had cherished against his own little brother."[12]

Whenever we feel we are better than other men, friendship is doomed. Whenever we look down or up to other men rather than eyeball to eyeball, chances of true brothering are diminished. Returning to school reunions, for example, we have difficulty restoring bonds that haven't been cultivated for twenty years. There is truth for men in the aphorism: "It is agreed by all that the two happiest periods of a man's life are his boyhood and about ten years from now."

I have only a couple of male friends from my childhood. I know that isn't the case with all men, but my male buddies tend to be comprised of the men with whom I live, move, play, work and grow — right here, right now.

Male friendship is a crucial component of my present life and meets needs not filled by my wife, family, or female associates. Friendship may be the most "religious" (that which binds us together again) act we men pursue. Stuart Miller in the best book available on male friendship writes:

Bold acts of consciousness are, I think, the true basics for an art of friendship these days. No gimmicks will work. The acts of friendship we need are inner acts, acts of the depth of the heart, of self-searching, and of decision.

Inwardly accepting the necessity to give friendship one's closest attention and recalling the social obstacles to friendship are the two basic inner acts.[13]

It's never easy and it's never too late to grow male friendships of singular worth and sustaining power. When Kahlil Gibran wrote, "and let there be no purpose in friendship save the deepening of the spirit," he reminds men yet again that brothering (or intimacy) and spirituality (or ultimacy) can be intertwined.

We spend ample time in our Brother-Spirit groups trying to talk about and develop deeper bonds with other men. Certain questions have proven nourishing:

1) How do you spend time with your male buddies?
2) Do you desire to travel deeper emotionally and spiritually with them?
3) Would you call any of them good, dear, or close friends?
4) What are your bedrock fears and hopes in your brother relationships?
5) When does someone become your soul-brother?

Blood Brothers

> Sisters are certainly the most satisfactory relations. They are your own age, which your children are not, and they are your own sex, which your husband is not, and they are your blood relations, which your friends are not. No one else can fill the gap.
>
> — spoken by Mary Thomas in James
> Thomas Flexner's *An American Saga*

Mary Thomas' words about sisters apply equally to brothers. I have only one sibling, a brother, and I am fortunate to announce that our love is real and deep and has weathered distance and lapses, as well as occasional squabbles and jealousy. He is my longest-standing male friend. When our mother dies, Phil will have known and cared about me longer than anyone else on earth.

There are precedents for blood-brother friendship. There was just one man who appreciated Vincent Van Gogh during his life, who encouraged, even underwrote, his painting career with affection and cash. The one painting Van Gogh sold during his lifetime was to his beloved brother, Theo. In the preface to *Dear Theo,* the autobiography of Vincent Van Gogh, we find:

> Each night, when the fourteen to sixteen hours of
> drawing and painting were over, Vincent sat down with
> pen and ink and poured out his heart to Theo. There was
> no idea or thought too small, no happening too trivial,
> no element of his craft too insignificant, no scene too
> unimportant for Vincent to communicate to the only
> other living person who considered his every word and
> feeling precious.[14]

A contemporary, touching brother-brother bond is that of John
Edgar Wideman, a college professor and prize-winning novelist, and
his blood brother, Robby, sentenced to life imprisonment for armed
robbery and murder. In his poignant account entitled *Brothers and
Keepers,* John writes: "Robby was inside me. Wherever he was, run-
ning for his life, he carried part of me with him."[15]

Another example of the blood-brother tie is provided in a sensitive piece by Dick Shaap about his relationship with his brother Bill,
entitled "My Brother, My Self":

> I do not really know my brother. I do not see him often
> or speak to him regularly, even though we live in the
> same city and we both make our living with words. We
> both consider ourselves to be, above all else, journalists,
> and yet, professionally, our paths almost never cross, and
> we rarely turn to each other for either advice or criticism.
> We are not close, not in any customary sense of the word,
> and yet I love him very much and admire him immensely
> and, even though I hardly ever read his writings, I take
> fierce pride in almost everything he does. I do not think
> this is because we sprang from the same womb, and share
> the same genes and memories. I think it is more because
> he is the me I once wanted to be, the me I might have
> been, the me I'll never be.[16]

Some reflections on my bond with my brother Phil. We go back,
yet ever forward, in history together. The term "brotherly love" was
meant for us. He is my buddy until death do us part. He is irreplace-
able in my life.

When Phil reached 50, I decided to fly him out to San Diego from
Topeka, Kansas and have the two of us do a musical concert. Even though
we had never sung a duet together, I was confident it would be an un-
abashed triumph of kinship, because we love one another fiercely and
enduringly. We dwell in concert with one another.

It was an evening of music, memories, and merriment. We shared our story of brotherly affection through familiar and original songs, conversation, audience participation, capped off with punch and birthday cake. Phil had flown out unannounced to sing at my 20-years-of-ministry celebration some years back. Now I was returning the favor in saluting my only "bro" — psychotherapist, consultant, composer, singer, and "magician of lyrical truths."

It was an adult evening for men and women, singles and partners, for all who joyously toast the stimulation and uplift of *kinship*.

It turned out to be one of the most emotionally rewarding and spiritually cementing events of my life. It exceeded my wildest hopes. Phil was ecstatic; our entire family reveled in the experience; my friends treasured meeting my brother. It was schmaltzy yet authentic. If Phil and I never spoke another word to one another, if one of us dropped dead, *dayenu* — it would be enough. It was enough.

Let me close discussion of this theme with an Hasidic Tale which I told at the beginning of our "Brothers in Concert":

> Two brothers — one a bachelor, the other married — owned a farm whose fertile soil yielded an abundance of grain. Half the grain went to one brother and half to the other.

> All went well at first. Then, every now and then, the married man began to wake with a start from his sleep at night and think: "This isn't fair. My brother isn't married, he's all alone, and he gets only half the produce of the farm. Here I am with a wife and five kids, so I have all the security I need for my old age. But who will care for my poor brother when he gets old? He needs to save much more for the future than he does at present, so his need is obviously greater than mine."

> With that he would get out of bed, steal over to his brother's place, and pour a sackful of grain into his brother's granary.

> The bachelor brother too began to get the same attacks. Every once in a while he would wake from his sleep and say to himself: "This simply isn't fair. My brother has a wife and five kids and he gets only half the produce of the land. Now I have no one except myself to support. So is it just that my poor brother, whose need is obviously greater than mine, should receive exactly as much as I

do?" Then he would get out of bed and pour a sackful of grain into his brother's granary.

One night they got out of bed at the same time and ran into each other, each with a sack of grain on his back!

Many years later, after their death, the story leaked out. So when the townsfolk wanted to build a temple, they chose the spot at which the two brothers met, for they could not think of any place in the town that was holier than that one.[17]

MAKING PEACE WITH THE EARTH

> Humankind has not woven the web of life. We are but
> one thread within it. Whatever we do to the web, we do
> to ourselves. All things are bound together. All things
> connect. Whatever befalls the Earth befalls also the
> children of the Earth.[18]
>
> — Chief Seattle's address to the
> American President, 1855

We men suffer from "andro-centrism," the belief that we are the
center of the universe and that God "has given man dominion over
the Earth to do with as he saw fit." This view has led to our rape of
the Earth.

Since men have been integrally involved in the devastation of our
ecosphere, we have a major responsibility to join the "deep ecology"
movement to become healers of the Earth and all its inhabitants.

From the book of Genesis, with its divine confirmation of creation as "good" and "very good," to the tender tradition of the Native American people, the religions of the world teach that the Earth
is a wondrous, holy place. Yet never before in human history have
violations of such magnitude threatened our planet and its children.

It is time for men to become our environment's keeper, brothers of
compassion and mercy to the life which surrounds, supports, and sustains our very beings. As Sam Keen relates in his new book on men:

> I know of no single honorific that defines a man so much
> as the verb "to husband." The verb is at once genderal
> and nongenital. A husbandman may or not plow and sow
> crops, but he certainly must take care of the place with
> which he has been entrusted. To husband is to practice
> the art of stewardship, to oversee, to make judicious use
> of things, and to conserve for the future.
>
> The image is as central to gay men, bachelors, and
> widowers living in high-rise apartments as to married or

landed householders. Psychologically, the husbandman is a man who has made a decision to be in place, to make commitments, to forge bonds, to put down roots, to translate the feeling of empathy and compassion into an action of caring.[19]

We meditate upon four basic questions in our Brother-Spirit circle attempting to raise our consciousness, acknowledge our interconnectedness, and become stewards in caring for our cosmos.

I. What experiences in your relationship with nature have been exhilarating, frightening, calming or . . . ?

More mystical experiences come to men in relationship to nature, plants, and animals than in any other guise. This is a stunning paradox in light of our treatment of the planet. Yet we men are torn creatures: we revel in the Earth's beauty and mystery *and* we abuse it. Both/and.

I invite us to follow in the compassionate footsteps of St. Francis who, while living communally with the brothers of his order, remained close to the Earth as well. It is told that he lived for blocks of time in a cave where he communed at length with the animals, which he addressed as "brothers."

II. Do you believe animals have feelings?

What have you learned from animals?
What would your life be like without animals?
What does it mean to talk about "equality of being?"
Where do you stand with respect to animals' rights?

This set of questions deserves an entire weekend. In John Seed and Joanna Macy's book, *Thinking Like a Mountain: Towards a Council of All Beings,* they map out a workshop where men and women wrestle with these questions. The primary aim of their Council is clear: "To enhance human commitment and resources for preserving life upon our planet home." They describe their vision of deep ecology as follows:

> In contrast to reform environmentalism which attempts only to treat some of the symptoms of the environmental crisis, deep ecology questions the fundamental premises and values of contemporary civilization . . .

Within the framework of deep ecology, and contrary to
key assumptions of Judaic/Christian/Marxist/humanist
tradition, humans are not to be viewed as the ultimate
measure of value or as the crown of creation. We are but
"a plain member" of the biotic community and our
arrogance with respect to this community threatens not
only ourselves but all of life. We must learn to "let beings
be," to allow other species to follow their separate
evolutionary destinies without dominating them. We
must come to understand that life-forms do not constitute a pyramid with our species at the apex, but rather a
circle where everything is connected to everything else.
We must realize that the environment is not "out there,"
and that when we poison the air or the water or the soil,
we poison ourselves because of the vast biological cycles
within which we too are inextricably embedded.[20]

III. Do you feel kinship with the soil, rocks, plants, sky, sea . . . ? In what ways?

IV. What does an Earth-centered spirituality mean to you?

What remains for you to do or be as a partner in "the interdependent web of existence"?

More and more brothers are confessing that the closer and kinder
they grow with nature, the more grounded they become with themselves and the gentler they behave with the men, women, and children who surround them.

There are other encouraging signs. One of the premier thinkers
of a new, earthy masculinity is Shepherd Bliss who defers to nine-
teenth-century naturalist Henry David Thoreau who said: "In short,
all good things are wild and free. . . . Give me for my friends and
neighbors wild ones, not tame ones." Bliss contends that unneces-
sary harm is done by contrasting Father-Sky and Mother-Earth and
quotes Arthur and Libby Colman in their book, *The Father: Mythology and Changing Roles,* who trace:

> . . . two archetypes of the earth and sky, affirming the
> Earth Father who has been underground for very long —
> yet remains in our memory in various forms such as
> Johnny Appleseed. The Colmans write, "There are many

earthy male figures who are protectors of the forest, gods
of the woods, streams and fields."

And there are various spiritual traditions which honor the
Earth Father. Geb the Egyptian is completed by Nut the
Goddess of the Night Sky. Shou-Lao, the Chinese god of
longevity, is associated with the generativity of the Earth
in his role as preserver of life.[21]

Bliss goes on to remind us that the Earth is not male or female:

The Earth has no gender. It is the source of All. Or it is
both genders, and more united in the One. No gender,
race, or people can lay exclusive claim to it. We all belong
to the Earth, not merely as mother, which is only half of
creation. Without the sacred phallic energy, there is no
divine birth, no divine child.[22]

We close our Brother-Spirit session on ecology with an Animal
Blessing:

Blessed are you, O God,
Maker of all things great and small.
On the fifth and sixth days of creation
You called forth fish from the sea, birds from the air
And animals from the land.
You inspired Francis of Assisi to call all animals
Sisters and brothers.
By the power of your love, enable them to live
    according to your plan.
May we love and cherish them,
For they are gifts of your love.
Blessed are you, O God, in all your creatures.
Amen, blessed be! [23]

HONORING OUR GOD

One can hardly do justice to the reality of God in one section. Whenever this book touches upon "ultimacy," it touches upon divine mystery in one shape or another. I have often taken brothers through a six-week series, entirely devoted to God-cepts and allowing for ample reflection and response:

Week One: God as Beginning, Source, and Creator

Week Two: God as Process, Middle, and Partner

Week Three: God as Aspiration, Beyond, and End

Week Four: God as Many and One

Week Five: God as Light and Dark

Week Six: God as Female and Male

I generate springboard quotes for each dialogue. A single Brother-Spirit circle engages the following questions:

I. What are the names/meanings of god/God in your life?

Three purposes here. First, this question forces us to consider a pluralism of concepts rather than hugging or feeling trapped by one deity. This question gives latitude. Second, some men consider God a capital Presence, others work more co-operatively with divinity in the "lower case." Third, the real charge in Brother-Spirit is never to define God in abstract terms but to describe God in your particular existence.

As J. A. T. Robinson once wrote:

> God is intellectually superfluous, emotionally dispensable, morally intolerable yet inescapably real as a subject in encounter.[24]

A concomitant question gives breathing room for the atheist or agnostic among our brothers: If the term God is meaningless to you, what is of ultimate value/worth/power in your life? No man, whatever his relationship to God might be, can avoid authentic responses to that question.

The religious challenge is equally concerned with God and the good, with the ethical and mystical, with forging intimate relations and following our vision of the ultimate, with the doable and unsayable. In Brother-Spirit we must wrestle with both moral imperatives and divine inscrutability.

II. The saints used to ask: "Whose am I? To whom do I belong?" Comment.

We men are quick to focus on who we are as male human beings, but our spiritual odyssey is incomplete if we fail to address the contextual, universal concern: Whose am I? How does our soul relate to the Oversoul, to use eastern religious language?

III. What power(s) — either human or divine, immanent, transcendent, or both — sustain you in your life? To whom/what do you turn during the dark nights of your soul?

It is too easy to answer simply "yes" or "no" to the classic query: "Do you believe in God?" This question doesn't push us far or wide, whereas questions like the ones above drive brothers into deeper waters. As do questions like these: What is your ultimate commitment in life? What holds you together? To what/whom do you give your loyalty?

IV. If meditation is primarily reaching within and prayer is reaching beyond, when and how do you engage in these exercises?

Brothers need options in the exposition of our sacred odyssey. Some of us are temperamentally unsuited for either meditation or prayer. But when granted a range of ways of relating to divinity, we usually discover a spiritual discipline that fits us.

To close this theme on "Honoring Our God," I would share sample quotes concerning God which can serve as creative catalyzers for additional Brother-Spirit conversation.

The Tao that can be spoken is not the eternal Tao.

— Lao Tzu

Thou canst not see my face; for there shall no one see me and live.

— Exodus 33:20

God is that power within us and within all life by virtue of which it is possible for us to love.

— Harry Meserve

When I am asked if I believe in God, I am either impatient or amused and frequently decline to reply. All I know, all I want to know is that I have found in my relations with my neighbors and in my glad beholding of the universe a reality to make my life as best I can a dedication to this reality.

— John Haynes Holmes

I call God mother and I call God father and I know that God is both and God is neither. I know that God is great beyond my imagination.

— Elizabeth Ellis Hagler

I don't say that God is one grand laugh, but I say that you've got to laugh hard before you can get anywhere near God.

— Henry Miller

The creed of the English is that there is no God and that it is wise to pray to God from time to time.

— Alisdair MacIntyre

Whatever the queer little word, God, means, it means something we can none of us quite get away from, or at; something connected with our deepest explosions.

— D. H. Lawrence

Concepts about God are only ways of explaining God and do not really touch the existence of God which is beyond knowing.

— George Marshall

I tend to be wary of "professional atheists." They·spend a little too much time thinking about God.

— Peter Christiansen

You cannot love God with your parents' heart.

— Solomon Schechter

I said to the almond tree, "Sister, speak to me of God." And the almond tree blossomed.

— Nikos Kazantzakis

BECOMING GOOD FATHERS AND GOOD SONS

> There is no absolute correlation between "good" father-
> ing and "good" children. There are too many factors at
> work. [25]
>
> — Arthur and Libby Colman

> We cannot save, be saved, but we can stand
> Before each presence with gentle heart and hand;
> Here in this place, in this time without belief,
> Keep the channels open to each other's grief . . . [26]
>
> — May Sarton

Earlier, I focused on the father-son bond using biblical examples of both heavenly and earthly interactions. This primal dyad of father-son yearns for further exploration in our Brother-Spirit journey. The father-son relationship is claimed by men to be our most pivotal male bond to heal and celebrate — whether the figures involved are near or far, known or unknown, alive or dead.

We have spent entire workshops viewing and responding to multi-dimensional father-son movies such as *The Tribute, The Great Santini,* and *Dad.* I recently planned a father-son circle revolving around modern songs like "Cat's Cradle" (where sons recycle the wound and grow up to be just like Dad), "I've Got a Name" (where sons are "living the dream Dad kept hid"), "Teach Your Children" (where sons and fathers reveal their respective dreams and hells), and "Leader of the Band" (where the son thanks and expresses deep love for his father and owns his position as "the living legacy to the leader of the band"). Such programs inspire men to compose poems, letters, or music from their depths of anguish and reconciliation.

There is no single, more pressing or poignant issue in men's lives than facing their fathers anew. And as Anne Sexton reminds us brothers, "It doesn't matter who my father was, it matters who I remember he was."

The Father-Son Continuum

It is essential for men to perceive ourselves as sons and fathers, moving both ways on a continuum. Our tendency has been to describe the father-son encounter in rigid terms when such bonds are actually complex and fluid. The dynamic interplay between father and son reminds me of that clever riddle: "That man's father is my father's son. Who is it?" The answer: "me." Brothers need to be ambidextrous when moving on the father-son continuum.

Recognizing the subtle variations involved, I encourage brothers to work along a basic continuum ranging from ABUSE to ABANDONMENT to ALOOFNESS to AVAILABILITY to AFFIRMATION to AFFECTION. In our father-son odysseys we find ourselves somewhere, at different junctures, on that continuum. There are strange blends as well: fathers who are emotionally abusive yet physically affectionate; fathers who are aloof when others are around but readily available when alone with their sons; fathers who abandon their sons early on, then return later, anxious to shower their "boys" with affirmation.

The questions in our Brother-Spirit circles flow: Where on the continuum would you place your father-son relationship when you were born, a child, a teenager, a young adult, currently? If you are a father, where would you locate yourself on the continuum with respect to your own children, particularly your sons?

If we were to revisit the father-son ties in the Bible, we would be able to chart them all on the continuum. Cain, for example, received a doubly damaging dose: rejection from God, his heavenly father, and absence from Adam, his earthly father.

An overwhelming number of father-son dyads register on the negative end of the continuum: conflicted, injured, incomplete. The wounds between father and son run deep; the grief is occasionally unbearable.

There are myths conveyed in various cultural stories urging men to "kill your father," destroy any vestige of father-son connection, cut yourselves off from dad forever. This is an extreme measure, but sometimes an irreconcilable situation calls for last resorts.

Novelist Erica Jong phrases it this way in *Parachutes and Kisses:*

"Why do you think you're so destructive?" Isadora asked.

> "I mean, really? Is it only your relationship with your
> father? Don't get me wrong — I believe in that sort of
> thing. I think that a man who never slays his father, never
> grows up — as witness my last ex-husband, Josh — but
> why are you slaying yourself?" [27]

The same sentiment is reflected in the Buddhist admonition: "If you meet the Buddha on the road, kill him." This is a symbolic way of decisively separating ourselves from our fathers and creating our own identities. Psychotherapist Erich Fromm makes the same point in gentler fashion: "Eventually, the mature person has come to the point where we are our own mother and our own father." [28]

Poet Robert Bly remarked, in an interview with Bill Moyer entitled "A Gathering of Men," that it took him until he was forty-six years of age, and his father was ailing, before significant peace could be made between the two of them. When Bly and his father could no longer afford to shame one another, they were freed to begin loving one another. They made the arduous trek from abuse to affection.

As men engaged in Brother-Spirit quest, we remind each other that it is usually possible to heal the wounds and celebrate the ties between fathers and sons. There are no time constraints. We have until *both* of us are in the grave. We men have the capacity to transform, even if not transcend, relationships of abuse, abandonment, and aloofness into bonds of greater availability, affirmation, and affection.

But this process is rigorous and requires all the emotional bravery and spiritual stamina fathers and sons can muster. Our particular father-son histories must be forthrightly acknowledged, not romanticized, and our special hungers and hurts faced, not denied, before genuine durable progress can be made. Our father-son exchanges are too significant to succumb to quick, cheap conciliation.

The reality is that our fathers are not "nothing" and will never be "everything" we sons desire or need. Most fathers are "something" — able to deliver some example and some meaning to our lives as sons. When we make peace with that compromised yet realistic vision of fatherhood, we allow our fathers to be themselves as we become ourselves, bonded without being enslaved to one another.

Additionally, we sons must remember that our fathers are partial beings, as are we all, trapped by conditioning and the transgenerational web launched in father-son exchanges related in the biblical odyssey. Robert Bly makes this point when he writes about his own father:

> I began to think of him not as someone who had
> deprived me of love or attention or companionship, but
> as someone who himself had been deprived, by his
> mother or by the culture. This process is still going on.
> Every time I see my father I have different and compli-
> cated feelings about how much of the deprivation I felt
> with him came willfully and how much came against his
> will — how much he was aware of and unaware of. I've
> begun to see him more as a man in a complicated
> situation.[29]

It is important to realize that reconciliation will not always be initiated by sons. In Homer's *Odyssey*, the warrior-king Odysseus returns and reveals himself to his teenage son Telemachus: "I am that father whom your boyhood lacked and suffered pain for lack of. I am he." The story continues with Telemachus weeping as he flings his arms around his repentant, brave father. Would that there were more fathers willing to retrace their steps, return to their sons, ask for forgiveness, reunite.

Good Fathers — Good Sons

We call our Brother-Spirit circles "Becoming Good Fathers — Good Sons" for various reasons. First, even in the most impoverished of connections between father and son, there are invariably positive memories to be saluted. These "good" moments need to be re-membered, lest they fade amid the anguish.

I personally came of age as a young adult male when I realized that my father was neither "everything" nor "nothing" but "something." Men are startled when, upon reflection, we discover the good (not perfect) experiences in our oft-difficult adventures with Dad. I have seldom met a man whose father-son bonds weren't ambivalent, filled with both pleasure and pain.

Second, in Brother-Spirit, we contend that men live more by our aspirations than our actualities. Having the image of "good father" before us strengthens our resolve to say "thanks" to our fathers, flawed as they were, are, and ever will be. An ideal of goodness also gives us a goal to pursue as fathers ourselves.

Too many men become "addicted" to negative memories and visions of our fathers, never unlocking the power of either our anger or our affection, just wallowing in self-pity. As Jungian analyst James Hillman notes:

> As long as you complain about your negative fathers,
> you remain a son. Use the negative in your psyche
> as an initiator. . . . Souls choose their parents. Blame
> your father, but then go to the second step and use this
> scar tissue.[30]

Third, in one of our Brother-Spirit circles, we had a striking breakthrough when we realized that the father-son relationship is a dance, requiring effort and good will from both partners. As sons we too have been abusive as well as affirming toward our fathers through the years. We shape *and* we are shaped by the bond. Sons have a responsibility, equally important as fathers, in making the bond more truthful and gratifying. We are connected in hurt; we must be joined in restoration.

Jacob transmitted personalized blessings to each of his sons from his deathbed in the Old Testament. It would have been a beautiful surprise if his eleven sons had responded in kind.

Peter, a member of our Brother-Spirit fellowship, was complaining because he had never received his father's approval, a tragic yet common male plight. He was emotionally arrested in his development, desperately hungering for his father's blessing. The truth is that Peter may wait for eternity and never receive it, but if he would risk initiating communion with his father, some lovely sharing might occur.

Perhaps if Peter would dare to reach out to his father first, extending whatever blessing is genuine, then his father could be stirred to respond from his depths. There is no guarantee, only an opportunity.

I am perennially moved by reading Herbert Gold's splendid memoir-novel of his immigrant Jewish family. In *Fathers* the author writes:

> There was no moment of reconciliation between my
> father and me. We quarreled, we lived together, we
> remained in touch, we warred again on occasion, we
> made it up, we looked ahead, we walked carefully with
> each other, we were part of a family. One day I noticed

that the war with my father was over. I don't remember
when that day came. It came more than once. There
would still be quarrels, but we had agreed upon the lines
of power. We each had our territory. We could each
allow the other to live. We were allies.[31]

Divine and Human Fathers

Those men raised in strong religious traditions often have found
that we could fill deficits with our earthly fathers by projecting miss-
ing yet desirable qualities onto God, the heavenly father. A variation
on this theme occurred in my own life.

My father, "an intangibly good father" (Erik Erikson's phrase)
loved his two boys dearly and deeply, but not demonstrably. He was
the consummate provider, working in the "fields" day and night, but
rarely present to talk, play, and eat with his family. He was a care-
taker, not a caregiver. His sons needed both.

I hungered for more regular male touch, warmth, conversation
from my live Dad than he was able to furnish. He was a child of his
own era, a son of an aloof father. Coaches and cubmasters plugged
some of my holes, but God, as an omnipresent, nurturing father,
was the major adult male-surrogate during my days as a youngster.
God was present when my Dad was absent.

My father, because he was aloof yet affirming (a tormenting
paradox), was too shadowy a figure during my daily life to converse
with, let alone rebel against. We never really "knew" one another,
our deep-down hurts or hopes. Since my livelier exchanges were made
with Father-God, I had, in effect, grown emotionally closer to a
heavenly father than my earthly one.

I rebelled late, during my college years, and when I became more
autonomous, "my own man," it was initially in reaction to Father-
God not Father-Harold. I wrangled with God in a fierce, necessary
struggle to shape my separate identity. This was a painful, convo-
luted process, because I was preparing to be a minister and my theo-
logical-emotional upheaval caused concern among both faculty and
family members. Nonetheless, it was an essential evolution and now,
at mid-life, I can reconnect with Father-God from a more mature,
adult perspective, realizing our distinct boundaries.

Furthermore, it was only when I began to wrench myself apart from a symbiotic tie with God that I could see clearly the gaps, links, and possibilities with my earthly Dad. This was a soul-searching, anguishing time. I increasingly withdrew from my Dad, just as he had unwittingly withdrawn from Phil and me during our upbringing.

Finally, amid unresolved hurt and hunger, I wrote my Dad an epistle of reconciliation — declaring what we had, didn't have, might still have as father and son. I acknowledged his failings, personal achievements and dead ends, lost dreams and driving urges (as best I perceived them) and his genuine, though not easily expressed, affection for his wife and two sons.

I noted our missings and connections over the years. I confessed my shortcomings as well. I listed the ways in which I loved him, however incompletely.

He sent me a love letter in return. Our modest exchange of letters enabled us both to bond at a more authentic level. It sufficiently healed our history and strengthened each of us for facing our two remaining decades alone and together.

Dad carried my epistle in his suit pocket until the day he died. His letter is nestled amid my prized memorabilia and imbedded in my heart's memory.

Here are some examples of the questions we raise during this exploration of the divine and human fathers in our Brother-Spirit journey.

Has Father-God been a remote or nurturing figure in your life — remaining in the sky or visiting your earth-home? Have your image of heavenly father *and* your reality of earthly father embodied similar or different qualities? Have they served distinct functions in your evolution as a man? What male figures in your odyssey has God resembled, if any? What is the current status of your relationship with Father-God? With your earthly father?

Another related zone our men's fellowship has addressed is: What did Jesus, the idealistic son suffering his torment on the cross, mean when he cried to Father-God, "Why hast Thou forsaken me?" What relevance does the Nazarene's cry have to your sonship with either God or your Dad?

Becoming a Father

Often when men become biological fathers, adoptive fathers, or step-fathers, our attitudes toward our own fathers mature. We become more understanding and accepting. What changes have taken place in your relationship as a *son* since you became a *father?* Do any of your father's patterns of behavior as a parent repeat themselves in your own fathering?

I also encourage men to think about our father's father, reflecting upon any trans-generational habits embedded in your father-son nexus today.

Peace-Making Heretics

> Nor did I ever tell him how close to him I felt that
> night — that for a little while the concrete wall between
> father and son had crumbled away and I knew that we
> were two lonely people struggling to reach each other.[32]
>
> — Moss Hart

I always close meetings on "Becoming Good Fathers and Good Sons" with additional opportunities for peace-making. We *inherit* our fathers, but as adult males we can become *heretics* (literally choice-makers). We don't have to be constrained by the fates; we can make changes. We can choose to view our fathers with fresh eyes, reach out to them anew. We can decide to be different kinds of sons as well.

The questions for our Brother-Spirit quest are as follows: How can you make peace today with both yourself (as a son) and your father? Recognizing, as the Colmans say, that there is "no absolute correlation between 'good' fathers and 'good' children," can you release earlier, hurtful father-son episodes and keep them from contaminating your present life? Can you live with imperfect father-son and son-father bonds? Can you forgive everyone involved without forgetting anything experienced?

William Butler Yeats, on his 50th birthday, remarked that the purpose of life was essentially to bless and be blessed. So it is. Good fathers and good sons struggle to touch one another, afresh, to hallow the fragile, incomplete bonds we hold in common. Can we bless and be blessed, as sons and fathers?

Bonding As Brothers

Yet another way to heal the wounds with our fathers is for sons to build bridges with other men. We will only have one biological father; reunion may never be possible. So be it. As men we may need to focus primary time and energy upon healthy, gratifying alliances with our male peers, develop brother-to-brother bonds.

Such ties will never prove sufficient substitutes for the father-son relationship, but they are worthy and accessible avenues for sons to grow male affection and meaning in our lives.

The truth is that sons can be buddies with other brothers but not with God or Dad. A difference in history, size, and kinship will always remain. An "over-against-ness," which need not be alienating, will always produce a gulf between the generations. In fact, some father-son, God-human bonds are diminished when we try to be cozy. As sons, we can never become intimate with our fathers — close but not intimate. Intimacy is reserved for true equals, peers, brothers.

As brothers we can make a pledge to ourselves and others that we will not intentionally hurt or harm the Abels in our existence. We will refuse to sacrifice our Isaacs, however tempting the stakes and whoever makes the demand. We will love our Absaloms *now* instead of waiting to mourn them when they are gone.

MESHING SEXUALITY AND SPIRITUALITY

Sexuality and spirituality are not enemies but friends.[33]

— Donald Goergen

In the Old Testament the same word, "yadah," was used for knowing God as for knowing our mate. Orthodox Jews, when praying, rock back and forth, which translates as making love to the holy spirit. However, sexual intercourse is not equatable to mystical communion with the divine. Both experiences are exquisite, ineffable, and singular, but neither can do full justice to the other.

Yet it is often true that when partners are close to one another in every way, we feel near divine presence. Intimacy and ultimacy, sexuality and spirituality are profoundly intertwined in partnership at its finest.

In Brother-Spirit circles, men are slow to talk about sexuality because we are inexperienced in being open, sensitive, and vulnerable with respect to such an intimate topic. We are more comfortable in the world of locker-room lies, barstool bravado, and conquest chatter. This is what Bernie Zilbergeld discovered in his study, *Male Sexuality:*

> Men are extremely secretive about their sexuality. They may joke about sex, talk a lot about this or that woman's characteristics and how they'd like to get in her bed, and make many allusions to their sexual prowess, but, other than these bits of bravado, most men simply don't talk about sex to anyone. One of the cornerstones of the masculine stereotype in our society is that a man has no doubts, questions, or confusion about sex, and that a real man knows how to have good sex and does so frequently. For a man to ask a question about sex, thereby revealing ignorance, or to express concern, or to admit to a problem is to risk being thought something less than a man. Almost every man tends to think that all other men are having a better time sexually than he has. . . . This reinforces his idea that it's best to keep his mouth shut.[34]

Jim Nelson's trenchant volume entitled *The Intimate Connection: Male Sexuality, Masculine Spirituality* is essential reading for brothers wishing to bring sexuality and spirituality into meaningful alignment. Using several of his insights, I have framed questions which enable men to explore their sexuality imaginatively and tenderly.

I. Our male sexuality revolves around pervasive performance anxieties.

We are trained, from the start, to perform on the field, in the office, in the classroom, and in bed. Nelson puts it this way:

> For "successful" heterosexual intercourse, I must perform — have an erection, be potent. Impotence is a man's threat, always waiting in the wings while he is onstage. But whether sexual impotence has ever been a problem or not, the potency/impotency syndrome becomes symbolic of life itself for one conditioned in the masculine mode. The performance mode of life is always demanding, and failure always lurks in the shadows. Because it is a strenuous, anxious life, I get angry. And if my genital performance has become somehow symbolic of a whole way of life, at whom might I be angry? Woman surely deserves my anger, for is she not the one inviting me to perform?[35]

My questions are these. Must our sensual-sexual experiences include erections to be "successful"? If so, why? If not, why not?

II. We men are beset with envy as well as anxiety.

Our envy is real. We brothers realize that perhaps the supreme life-moment for women is giving birth to children and, since men are tangentially connected to that primal event, we feel like outsiders. Therefore, we are envious. Nelson reinforces this concern:

> Another quirk of the male psychological experience regarding women is envy. In spite of centuries of mistaken reproductive biological knowledge, men have always known that in the birthing process women are much more involved with life-giving than they. Birth is awesome, mysterious, powerful, and men have only a remotely connected role. Instead of Freud's theory of women's penis envy (a phenomenon more commonly encountered in the male locker room than in the female psyche), a theory of men's womb envy may be more appropriate.

How else can we understand the male symbols of our own birthing powers — the Father God gives birth to the Son, Adam gives birth to Eve, male clergy give birth to new life through baptism — symbols that many men still jealously guard? Envy breeds resentment. Envy of the womb breeds resentment of the one who has the womb. That the resentment is unconscious makes it no less real, only more devious.[36]

My questions are: How do men make the most of our given sexual physiology? What does it mean for us to be creative, recreative, procreative beings? How can we deal constructively with our "womb envy"?

Brothers find that just talking about our sexual anxiety and envy provides a giant step toward muting these demons.

III. Penis and Phallus

Nelson makes fruitful distinctions between our *penis*, "the organ in its flaccid, unaroused state," and *phallus*, "the organ in its erect state." He goes on:

In spite of the quantitative dominance of penis time, men tend to undervalue penis, and overvalue phallus. . . . We have been taught and have learned to value phallic meanings in patriarchy: bigger is better (in bodily height, in paychecks, in the size of one's corporation or farm); hardness is superior to softness (in one's muscles, in one's facts, in one's foreign policy positions); upness is better than downness (in one's career path, in one's computer, in one's approach to life's problems). In a "man's world," small, soft, and down pale beside big, hard, and up.[37]

I exhort brothers to envision that penis is as masculine (not underdeveloped or feminine) a reality as phallus. I ask us to believe that full, mature men are both soft and hard, gentle and firm, hanging back, sinking down, withdrawn sometimes as well as erect.

What are the non-sexual situations where brothers can benefit from being penile as well as phallic?

Nelson continues: "Without periods of genital rest, a man lacks phallic capacity. Without times of retreat to the desert, there is no greening." The question persists: How do men build "periods of genital rest" as well as spiritual sabbatical into our lives?

Instead of resisting our masculine sexuality we men need to find healthy, caring ways to fulfill it. For whole women want whole men, and vice versa. Our crisis as men is primarily internal and self-inflicted. We would do well to affirm both our penile and phallic natures.

Another male fear is the dark.

> But most men are less at home in the darkness than in the light. We are heirs of the Enlightenment, a male-oriented rational movement that sought to shed light on everything. Our psyches seem to link darkness with death, and fear of death is characteristic of the patriarchal society. . . . The penis, in contrast to the phallus, is a creature of the dark. It is resting. Asleep . . . Its quiescence seems symbolic of death, its limpness the reminder of male-dreaded impotence, and fears of death and impotence are the cause of much destruction. But without the darkness there is no growth, no mystery, no receptivity, no deep creativity. Without the gentle dark, light becomes harsh.[38]

This fear of darkness exhibits itself in various forms. Men are loath to be caught asleep on the job. Naps are for children. Yet the Taoist sage knows better:

> The Sage falls asleep not because he ought to, nor even because he wants to, but because he is sleepy.[39]

We desperately need, yet seldom take, Sabbaths. We are driven. We don't admit to being "petered out."

Nelson moves men toward wholeness by having us look at our genitalia in the fullest context — honoring both penis and phallus as sacred realities. When we dare to do so, our sexual sharing, our spiritual exploration, and our total lives are healthier and holier.

IV. Playfulness

In Brother-Spirit we take our sexual lives seriously but not grimly. Men are so goal oriented in work or sex that we forget that sexuality, at its finest and fullest, is for the foolish and funny, the clumsy and playful ones. As Robert Capon reminds men:

> Desire and drainage are hilariously close. That's a tip-off to take it lightly.[40]

We ask one another these questions as brothers committed to

the path of playfulness. What ways have you found to relax, surrender, be light hearted in your sexual communication with your partner? Do you engage in foreplay merely as a warm-up to sexual union or as an enjoyable experience per se? Can you play sensually and erotically with your lover without feeling impelled to relate genitally?

V. Trust

Our male sexuality and spirituality demand sufficient trust for deepening to transpire. Living in a technologically sophisticated world, men are partial to scientific values. In our pursuit of spiritual discipline we garner tools. In our sex education we are deluged with information and techniques.

But in our sexual-spiritual explorations men would do well to heed Carl Jung's sage advice: "Learn your theories well, but put them aside when you touch the miracle of the living soul." To trust our male or female partner means to reverence, respect, and handle them with abiding care.

Trust cannot be proved. There will be evidence, of course, in our sexual partnerships but never conclusive data to warrant trust. Rather, trust is a spiritual gamble, a leap of reasoned, courageous faith.

Henry Miller, in describing sexual intercourse, put it powerfully, as if he were speaking directly to the male condition:

> If you enter deep enough, remain long enough, you will
> find what you seek. But you've got to enter with heart
> and soul and check your belongings outside.

How can we men touch our partners with a more trusting spirit — with caressing rather than clutching or controlling hands and hearts? Are we confident enough of ourselves that we can give freely to another, and confident enough of our partners that we can trust them with our gift?

VI. Mystery

Finally, our sexual and spiritual lives as men are most satisfying when we pay heed to van der Leeuw's saying: "The mystery of life is not a problem to be solved, but a reality to be experienced."

Undeniably, our human sexuality is bathed in mystery, from beginning to end, and in treating it as such, men are freed from the burdensome responsibility of having to have the last word, of having to make perfect love. We are delivered from the impulse to play Superman or God relative to our sexual-spiritual journeys. We are freed to be simply and fully our male selves — a glorious and sufficient task for the remainder of our days.

In that freedom, nothing is ever sealed. Our brothering adventure continues; the mysteries are inexhaustible.

EXPLORING DEEP WISDOM

> Where is the Life we have lost in living? Where is the
> wisdom we have lost in knowledge? Where is the
> knowledge we have lost in information? [41]
>
> — T. S. Eliot

The mythopoetic approach of Robert Bly focuses on intuition and archetypal imagery rather than the rational and systematic thinking of traditional men. Bly and Jungian analysts Robert Johnson and James Hillman call this "deep masculinity."

This vision of the male psyche meshes with the progressive theology of Paul Tillich, who remarked midway in this century:

> Depth in its spiritual use has two meanings: it means
> either the opposite of "shallow" or the opposite of "high."
> Truth is deep and not shallow; suffering is depth and not
> height. Both the light of truth and the darkness of
> suffering are deep. . . . The name of this infinite and
> inexhaustible depth and ground of all being is God. If
> that word has not much meaning for you, translate it and
> speak of the depths of your life, of the source of your
> being, of what you take seriously without reservation, of
> your ultimate concern. They who know about *depth*
> know about God. [42]

Thus we have male poets, psychologists, and theologians focusing on *depth* (descent) rather than *height* (ascent) as the metaphor for describing the intimate and ultimate.

When men explore the depths, we open ourselves to our vulnerability, our dark, our hidden, our grief, yet our joy and our ecstasy as well. For too long the male personality and creativity have been associated with the abstract realm, the remote — the steeple in religion, the erection in sexuality, and the skyscraper in business.

Perched upon lofty locales, men exude arrogance. When we enter the depths of existence, we are in touch with our ground, the earth, the "humus" (as in humble). Depths beckon us on a mysterious yet nourishing quest; heights seduce us into more conquests.

A year ago our Men's Fellowship went on our semi-annual wilderness renewal into the Laguna Mountains just outside San Diego. Our theme was "Wisdom Born of Intimacy." We invited men to flaunt neither their intellects nor book learning but to draw instead upon inner truths born of tears and toil, dancing, anger, silence, and eros. We invoked the wisdom from our "intimata," the innermost parts of our beings, believing that wisdom and intimacy flow inexorably from one another.

We started a ritual of inviting two of our men, one young and one old, one gay and one straight, to stand before us at the beginning and close of each day and utter wise words to guide us on our paths. They were charged to speak the truth as they felt it. They were our designated sages for the weekend.

In the morning of our time together we accented three dimensions of wisdom: fear, discernment, and kindness.

I. Fear

"The fear of the Lord is the beginning of wisdom," wrote the Psalmist (111:10). Religion doesn't get out of the starting blocks without a healthy shot of "awe-fulness" — awe, as in wonder; awe, as in terror; awe, as in respect and reverence for a power beyond our creation, beyond our comprehension, and far beyond our control. A presence in which we live, move, and have our being.

Fear in the face of throbbing, raw reality. Fear before the transforming judgment and love of divine mystery. Fear that I am not everything I thought I was and fear that I may be more than I believe.

As open, vulnerable men our days and nights are filled with angst, but those who fear the Lord are in mighty good company.

Ponder the shepherds of old and their initial response of fear, great fear upon encountering a divine messenger out in the fields. They were shepherding, per usual, and were abruptly interrupted by an extraordinary event: an angel appeared, "the glory of the Lord shone around them," and the shepherds were "filled with fear."

We are so accustomed to hearing the comforting words: "Be not afraid, for behold, I bring you good news of a great joy . . . " that we forget the huge fear which these men felt and had to be soothed.

The shepherds were "sore afraid," reads the King James version. The New English Bible translates the phrase: "terribly afraid." The shepherds were not caught off guard, not unnerved, not beset with a mild anxiety attack, but "sore afraid," "filled with fear" — real scared.

Why? Frightened by the startling voice of a strange personage? Frightened by a power beyond their grasp, an event beyond their wildest anticipation? In any case, whatever the source, "they were sore afraid."

Now as we all know, there is a happy ending. Romance prevails. The fears of the shepherds were in fact allayed. They went with haste to Bethlehem, saw Mary, Joseph and the babe lying in a manger, were duly impressed, spread the good news and returned home . . . "glorifying and praising God for all they had heard and seen."

But not, however, before these men had to face full-fledged fear. So must brothers today, as we work in our respective fields.

I think of the Lutheran Seminary which in its catalogue lists a degree of Master of *Scared* Theology. A wise typo, for ministers spend our professions being both sacred and scared. And, yes, scarred as well.

After these opening reflections on "fear," the following questions were posed, answered personally, dialogued about in the larger circle.

What brings you, as a man, a healthy sense of fear in life?

Where are those places and presences before which you stand in awe, respect, are "sore afraid"?

Brothers have disclosed the various anxieties un-easing their lives:

— "My children may never understand, let alone appreciate, my life-work."

— "I am growing closer to men with fear and trembling."

— "I will quit being *driven* by my visions."

— "I am slipping out of alignment with God."

— "Women and I seem to be passing in the door."

II. Discernment

> God, grant us the courage to change the things we can change, the serenity to leave unchanged those things we cannot change, and the wisdom to know the difference.
>
> — Reinhold Niehbuhr

When we share this prayer, productive, hard-achieving men focus essentially on the first part of the prayer because we presume to be change-agents.

However, this prayer is not merely about change or even the lack of change in our lives, but primarily about the wisdom of knowing the difference between the two, about judgment, making distinctions, saying yes and no, about sifting, selecting, and shedding, about discernment.

Men, according to Ralph Waldo Emerson, are "importuned with emphatic trifles." The key is to know the difference between a mere trifle and an emphatic trifle, to let the one pass and to embrace the other.

Men race out to change the world, often in its entirety and in one fell swoop, but we leave our interior castles in disarray. Clergy are renowned for leaving intimates, family, and those nearest us famished for communion while we nourish the world at large. Hear the late-life lament of the great preacher John Haynes Holmes:

> Another time I would do my part, above all, by banishing
> from my heart that vanity which drew me away from my
> wife and children in pursuit of my career as preacher,
> lecturer, and orator in general.[43]

Our need as growing men is to practice the art of discernment. There are dual dangers of tranquilizing into "zombie-hood" as well as outracing the rats in the rat race. There must be sufficient amounts of unrest and peace, change and changelessness in our sacred quest.

What are the areas in your life where it would be wise for you as a man to risk changes? Now.

What are the things — traditions, aspects of personality, habits — that as a grown man you choose to keep? What are the unchangeables in your existence? What can you let go and let be in your life?

How do you know the difference between "I can" and "I can't" in your decision-making? What inspiration or sources of wisdom do you draw upon to help make crisp, incisive decisions?

A sage is a person of keen, farsighted, sound judgment. In your dyadic sharing tell your brother in what ways you seem to be a discerning man, a sage.

III. Kindness

It's not the homeless, the corrupt power-brokers, the world demagogues that tax and test our kindness the most in life. More than outsiders, it is invariably those nearest and dearest to us that drive men up and down walls. The ornery ones, the pugnacious ones, the grudge holders, the laggards, the disturbers of the peace, the unlovables right in our own circle of family, friends, and acquaintances. Such are the persons who press our kindness to the limit.

In Jewish tradition it is spoken simply and with unmistakable clarity in an old proverb: "The highest form of wisdom is kindness." If fear is the beginning of wisdom, then kindness is its highest form.

If any of our lives might be blessed enough to close out in a burst or gesture of kindness it would be right. For we men know that when in doubt, be kind; when frightened, risk kindness; when bitter, try kindness. To paraphrase St. Augustine: we can be kind to the universe and do as we please, for if we are being kind, we are religious, we are wise, our house is in order.

— Who are those near and far, known and foreign, familiar and strange toward whom wisdom calls you to be kind?

— When does your kindness become saccharine, spineless, self-serving?

— What are the non-human beings who clamor for your kindness?

In the afternoon we engaged in the wisdom gained from non-competitive, new games such as trust walks, infinity volleyball, human sculpture. We played like children, with a parachute, acted foolish and zany. It was delightful and reminded me of the passage in the New Testament where disciples came to Jesus asking who was the greatest and Jesus, in turn, equated greatness with being child-like, humble, innocent, trusting, playful.

We danced, free lance as well as in a circle, with drums beating, and invited each brother, as the spirit summoned, to move forward alone to the center of the circle and express himself in swirling declaration.

During another Brother-Spirit circle we focused on the "Many Faces of Wisdom." Our inspiration came from the short phrase in Luke 7:35 where Jesus contrasts his lifestyle with that of John the

Baptist, yet claims that each has its own merit, "for wisdom is justified by all her children." In short, wisdom has many faces, is disclosed in multiple forms. God uses persons of distinct gifts and attitudes like John the Baptist and Jesus of Nazareth. Wisdom is kaleidoscopic and can be fathomed through diverse guises and paths.

It is humbling for men, whenever we slide toward certitude, to realize that wisdoms arrive in various ways and we earthlings are to honor rather than rate the range of avenues. Joseph Priestley came by his truths via the scientific method, a thorough empiricism. William Ellery Channing claimed reason rather than revelation as the instrumental source of his faith. Margaret Fuller, as a Transcendentalist, contended that intuition was her entrée to the divine. Dorothea Dix found her religion verified in prophetic duty.

Where do you stand on the wisdom continuum? What is your primary mode of truth-seeking? Are you a scientist, rationalist, mystic, activist, or a blend?

Welcoming Wonder

> At twenty, stopping round about,
> I thought the world a miserable place
> Truth a trick, faith in doubt,
> Little beauty, less grace,
> Now at sixty, what I see,
> Although the world is worse by far,
> Stops my heart in ecstasy;
> God! the wonders that there are! [44]

> — Archibald MacLeish

My buddy Clarke Wells writes in *Sunshine and Rain at Once:*

> Once upon a time there was a magician who didn't know
> he was one because nobody ever told him he was. . . .
> (He) lived simply . . . and worked at his job hard as you
> would expect an ordinary man to work at an ordinary
> job. When one day he died it was an ordinary sort of
> death. . . .

> Some time after the funeral the magician's children
> discovered a diary which they did not know their father
> had kept, and they opened it and a jaguar jumped out,
> and yards and yards of rainbow silk, desperate, beautiful,
> unwinding.[45]

In every brother resides untold miracles. The challenge is for us to share our magic while alive, to open our pockets, our hearts, and let our wonders shine forth.

I have two admonitions for brothers on the spiritual path. First, I invite us to quit explaining the mysteries of life and start basking in astonishment. Life is not comprised of problems to be solved but wonders to be enjoyed. Second, I invite men to quit rushing and begin relaxing, to slow down and bathe ourselves in the beauty and wonder right in front of us.

First, some words on mystery. One of the most troubling things about our contemporary society is our quickness to scrub the world clean of mystery. That signals not a healthy sense of science but the work of scientism. As religious brothers our job is never to reduce life to the logical and literal, never to throw away symbol, ritual and myth, never to ignore what we cannot comprehend but to encounter and enjoy the marvelous stuff outside our beings.

We were born in mystery, live in the midst of it and will return to it upon our death. Blessed be mystery!

Even if future generations solve problem after problem, ethical and political as well as personal ones, there will remain unfathomable mysteries, things we humans can neither understand nor unravel.

Our job, while on earth is to plunge into mysteries: open ourselves to their perplexity and promise. Engage life, meet death, surrender to love, wrestle with evil.

So I ask our brothers: What do you find mysterious in life? Be as specific and as inclusive as possible, delving into interior marvels as well as natural mysteries. Nikos Kazantzakis' novel, *Zorba the Greek,* is a story of intimacy and ultimacy where issues of friendship and wonder are beautifully interwoven. Here is one instance of Zorba's sense of wonder as recounted by the Boss:

> . . . like the child, Zorba sees everything for the first time. He is forever astonished and wonders why and wherefore. Everything seems miraculous to him, and each morning when he opens his eyes he sees trees, sea, stones and birds, and is amazed.
>
> "What is this miracle?" he cries. "What are these mysteries called: trees, sea, stones, birds?"
>
> One day, I remember, when we were making our way to the village, we met a little old man astride a mule. Zorba opened his eyes wide as he looked at the beast. And his look was so intense that the peasant cried out in terror.
>
> I turned to Zorba.
>
> "What did you do to the old chap to make him cry out like that?" I asked him.
>
> "Me? What d'you think I did? I was looking at his mule, that's all. Didn't it strike you, boss?"
>
> "What?"

"Well . . . that there are such things as mules in this world!" [46]

What are the strange, marvelous things in your world that turn your head, startle your heart, lift your spirit? Let your brothers in on your secret wonders.

It is satisfying for us to behold the mule, the lilies, the moon, the sunset, but what about the tornado and earthquake? We cannot wrench beauty from the whole. We live in an interdependent web of existence, and the web isn't always a pleasant reality. Everywhere we roam in the universe we experience wonders full of harshness and pain. Name some of those demonic wonders in your life.

My second admonition to our brothers is this: let's stop racing around and by the wonders of our days and slow down to smell some roses.

As the great Jewish philosopher Abraham Heschel said upon his deathbed: "I did not ask for success; I have asked for wonder. And you, God, have given it to me!"

The creation is filled with wonder, my brothers, but you and I must grasp it, experience it, revel in it.

When any brother asks: What is the meaning of life? I repeat the reply of the Zen Master who attained enlightenment and wrote lines to celebrate it:

> Oh, wondrous marvel:
> I chop wood!
> I draw water from the well! [47]

HEALING OUR WOUNDS

The wound that can be named can be healed.[48]

— John Stokes

Healing is a particularly pressing concern for men because it is hard for us to admit our wounds and seek help when hurt. Adult male lives are full of sores, open and closed. Our bones and hearts have been broken repeatedly.

Men's wounds are deep and varied. Some men are injured by the rigid roles society has "imposed" upon them from early childhood. Others are ashamed about their participation, personally and institutionally, in oppressing women and hurting children. Still others are disgusted with self-inflicted wounds.

As Albert Schweitzer said: "The largest fellowship in the world is those who bear the mark of pain." As bearers of emotional, physical, and spiritual scars men belong to this fellowship.

It goes unacknowledged that Jesus spent twenty percent of his ministry in healing wounds and one percent in espousing moral principles. His was a ministry of unswerving compassion and those who heal are authentic extensions of his mission. As poet Ric Masten says in "The Second Coming":

> go!
> tell the Catholics
> tell the Protestants
> the Millenium is here!
> at long last
> God has acknowledged
> two thousand years
> of prayers prayed
> Jesus has reappeared
> in all his glory!
> i know
> because i saw him

at the Hospice
tenderly washing the feet
of a man who was dying
of AIDS [49]

I. In what ways are you currently healing or recovering from your infirmities, be they emotional, physical, spiritual, intellectual, or relational?

Brothers are willing to open old wounds and address new ones. We talk about lost dreams, former partners, abandoned children, and abusive parents. We acknowledge that wounded animals are the most dangerous, so we must tend to our own wounds or we will be of little healing value to others. In the healing process we struggle to move beyond vengeance and blame, to say farewell to the past and greet our futures with forgiving eyes. We resonate with the biblical beatitude: "Blessed are they who mourn, for they shall be comforted."

One key for men is to recognize that healing is an ongoing process. We never fully recover; we remain in a state of recovering from whatever addiction, abuse, alienation, or ailment we might suffer. We are recovering workaholics, sexists, homophobics, racists, and so much more. We reside on a continuum from "dis-ease" to wellness. Ever on the path, ever reforming, ever healing.

II. What are the wounds you have inflicted upon others and which hanker for healing?

Be they major or minor, past or present, every brother I have ever met has an ample supply of wounds he has administered and from which he wishes to be cleansed. We are both wounded and wounders. None of us rests at ease.

If our personal lives are in order, then we are likely to be perpetrators of social injustices which need redress. We may feel at one with God, but our kinship with the animals and plants may be out of kilter. Brothers are called to be active healers on every front: internal, interpersonal, and international. The tragedy is that fratricidal behavior has been globalized. Our killing Abel is related to our killing strangers today in other lands.

Men need to repent and declare unequivocally that no country, no government, no military, no people has a right to contemplate, let alone prepare for, genocide. Such a policy is blatantly unconscionable. American men have grown up conditioned to treat our enemies as faceless creatures.

Yet we can no longer believe in a world of absolute good (us) and absolute bad (our foes). We must stay at the table with our alleged opponents and see them not so much as "enemies," but as "strangers" we do not know.

There is a Talmudic legend that says a traveler came at twilight to a campsite. Looking off into the distance he saw a strange object which seemed to be shaped like a monster through the gathering dusk. Though fearful, he mustered resolve, drew nearer and discovered that it was a man, which caused a great deal of his fright to vanish. Venturing still closer he found it was not only a human like himself, but it was his own brother!

This story captures the wound, fear, and challenge of our era. As Quaker philosopher Douglas Steere phrases it:

> When Joseph's brethren were given the terms of their receiving further grain to save them and their families from the famine in Israel, they were told that they must produce their younger brother Benjamin, who had remained at home. Joseph is said to have put this into words that God may be speaking to us today: "Except you bring your brother with you, you shall not see my face." [50]

Unless brothers are brave enough to face our enemies forthrightly and compassionately, we will be unable to face God.

There is an apt saying on the walls of a Spanish harbor:

> I am seeking God, but I do not find God. I am seeking myself but I do not find me. But I do find my neighbor and the three of us get on our way together.

III. The New Testament raises a provocative question for us men in this healing parable from John (5:2-9):

> Now there is in Jerusalem by the Sheep Gate a pool, in Hebrew called Bethzatha, which has five porticoes. In these lay a multitude of invalids, blind, lame, paralyzed. One man was there, who had him and knew that he had been lying there a long time, he said to him, "Do you want to be healed?" The sick man answered him, "Sir, I

have no man to put me into the pool when the water is
troubled, and while I am going another steps down
before me." Jesus said to him, "Rise, take up your pallet,
and walk." And at once the man was healed, and he took
up his pallet and walked.

It seems a foregone conclusion that we all want wholeness. What
a strange, demeaning question from the lips of our brother Jesus!
Upon further reflection, I'm not so sure that it was wrong of Jesus to
ask this invalid of thirty-eight years: "Do you want to be healed?"

Some men have done all we can to rehabilitate or cure our illness. Others of us are like the paralytic in the story who has been
unable or maybe unwilling (decimated by doubt or depression) to
do anything about our illness. We have not been sufficiently committed to the healing process. Consequently we have languished,
unhealed, for eons.

Lots of men carry around pent-up anger, agony, and ache not
merely for months, but for years, decades, lifetimes. Think of our
psychological and spiritual wounds for a moment. When we don't
release on them, we become increasingly crippled or paralyzed as a
result, what Robert Raines calls "in-valid."

What parts of you do you want to be healed? Which parts do
you choose to remain unhealed? These are painful yet real questions.

Brothers, think of your responses not only in terms of your body
or soul, but also with respect to societal breaks, hurts, and illnesses
we are not ready to heal. What are those situations where you choose
quietism over confrontation, "status quo-ism" over reform?

The sick man answered Jesus, "Sir, I have no one to put me into
the pool when the water is troubled, and while I am going down
another steps before me." All of that is probably true. There are undoubtedly even more reasons why he hasn't gotten into the pool for
thirty-eight years. Some of them are bona fide reasons and others are
lousy excuses. Some are "I can'ts" and others are "I won'ts." Jesus is
pressing to help the man sort out which are which and see if healing
is possible, even desirable.

It is no surprise that my mother's cancer recovery group, launched
by Norman Cousins, is named: "We Can Do!" Studies show that up
to ninety percent of patients who reach out for medical help are suffering from self-limiting disorders well within the range of the body's

own healing powers. The truth is that patient participation in healing is no longer an extra but an imperative.

Deeply respectful of our human capacity, even in our invalidism, to take some responsibility for our lives and share in our own healing, Jesus said, "Rise, take up your pallet, and walk." And the man did. In our healing we are agents, not victims.

"Do you want to be healed?"

IV. Another germinal phrase in the New Testament is "Physician, heal yourself." (Luke 4:23)

High-performing, hard-working men are proficient at taking care of other people's problems without addressing our own. Overweight male doctors are seen prescribing nutritional programs for patients. Spiritually deficient ministers urge parishioners to undertake devotional practices. On and on run the examples. The harsh truth is that men in the "helping professions" are living frauds until we work on our own wellness.

Joseph Jastrab, a leader in guiding vision quests for men, was interviewed in *Wingspan: A Journal of the Male Spirit.* He said:

> The most censored, most ignored story of our times is the story of men's suffering. Until that story is fully told by men and heard by both men and women, the medicine contained within a man's "seed" will be forever impotent. But it is precisely the tears released as the story is told and witnessed that moisten the hard seed coat, initiating [a] rooting into the earth; that is an act of love, an act of courage.[51]

Men are often conflicted beings within ourselves and notorious for inflicting wounds on our own flesh and soul in addition to outsiders. We need to clean up our own households first. In the book *Beyond Patriarchy: Essays by Men on Pleasure, Power and Change,* Michael Kaufman talks honestly about men's violence against ourselves:

> When I speak of a man's violence against himself I am thinking of the very structure of the masculine ego. The formation of an ego on an edifice of surplus repression and surplus aggression is the building of a precarious structure of internalized violence.[52]

During the course of this circle on healing I have brothers go to different quiet spots in our sacred meeting space, close our eyes and chant repeatedly the phrase: "Physician, heal thyself." We return to the larger group after ten minutes of chanting and share our feelings.

As brothers we constitute a supportive community for one another. We acknowledge the incessant struggles with illness and healing within ourselves and among us all. We do not judge, chastise or pass out cheap palliatives to one another. We attempt to be contagious carriers of honesty and compassion.

Robert Ingersoll once remarked that, had he been God, he would have made health contagious instead of disease. I understand Ingersoll's complaint, but it's not the whole story, for health too *can* be contagious. Despite our wounds and warts, we brothers are called to become authentic healers, to share wellness through words, presence, touch.

We also need to be respectful that brothers will choose variant ways of healing. What works for you may not for Hal or Bert or Al. Rabbi Nachman once wrote: "God calls one person with a shout, one with a song, one with a whisper."

There's a cartoon of a bearded guy walking the streets with a placard which says: "The world is not coming to an end; so we will just have to suffer and learn to cope." He's right. We have neither a clear-cut paradise nor a full-fledged hell on earth; it is a messy mix of the two.

Until life closes out, and who knows when that's going to happen personally or globally, we brothers keep on keeping on, coping and struggling the best we can, both receptive and resistant to healing, wounded healers, partially recovering of body, mind, and soul.

FACING DEATH AND BEYOND

> Had the religions of the world developed through her
> mind, they would have shown one deep, essential
> difference, the difference between birth and death. The
> man was interested in one end of life, she in the other.
> He was moved to faith, fear, and hope for the future; she
> to love and labor in the present.[53]
>
> — Charlotte Perkins Gilman, in
> *His Religion and Hers*

Gilman's distinction comes as no surprise, given women's natural, dominant role in procreation and men's fascination with death, due to the pre-eminent place we've played in war and its variations. Danaan Parry in his essay "We're Not Ready Yet, But Soon" writes:

> I have talked to so many Vietnam vets, my brothers who
> have experienced kill and/or be killed. They, most of
> them, ache. They are lost. And they whisper to me of a
> terrible awareness that on the battlefield, facing probable
> death, they felt, for the first time in their life, fully alive.
> And every experience since then has had a meaningless
> mediocre taste to it. How are we to make sense of all this?
> And we *must!*[54]

Brother-Spirit is trying to forge a new understanding of our male sexuality and place in the procreative process. So also, sensitive men aspire not to be death-defiers or death-bringers but confronters of death as a holy force, to be handled with exceeding care and awe.

Elie Wiesel cautions us against glorifying death as he recalls an Old Testament legend:

> When all is said and done, Joshua's wars are presented
> as wars, not as religion. His book about war is a book
> against war, a tale of bloodshed to teach resistance to
> bloodshed.
>
> When King Nebuchadnezzar of Babylon, who destroyed

the Temple, felt the urge to sing, the angel Michael
slapped him in his face. Destruction and singing do not
go together.

When the Jews crossed the Red Sea, the angels felt like
singing, and God told them to keep quiet: "My creatures
are drowning and all you can think about is singing!"

But then, if God cared that much about the Egyptians,
why did He drown them? That is for Him to answer. But
the angels were wrong to use the death of human beings —
however wicked — for purposes of lyrical theology. Death
must never be glorified. [55]

I. If you could choose, in what manner would you prefer to die?

Men become engrossed in this question, even so far as to depict
their death scene and feelings in detail.

A follow-on question would be: Who do you want to be by your
side at your time of departure?

Another one: What needs to happen for you to die with dignity?

II. How have the deaths of others affected you?

Sometimes our focus on death gets egocentric. The following
questions stir men to deal with memories larger than their own egos
by paying allegiance to other people besides themselves.

In the play "I Never Sang For My Father," there is the telling
line: "Death ends a life but not a relationship which struggles on in
the survivor toward resolution."

Are there individuals who are dead with whom you still need to
make peace? Are you willing to do it? How?

The dead end up being not only those we knew, loved, or de-
spised but figures we never met (grandparents who died before we
were born) or famous individuals we would cherish meeting like
Beethoven. What would you like to say to these persons whom you
never knew personally?

III. What do you believe happens to you (body, spirit, influence) after you die?

Make notes and share them with your brothers.

IV. How did Jesus grieve?

When Jesus' dear comrade, John the Baptist, was beheaded, and he learned of the tragic death, Jesus grieved. "Now when Jesus heard this, he withdrew from there in a boat to a lonely place apart." (Matthew 14:13)

Each of us needs to deal with loss in a private fashion. When we fail to take seriously Jesus' example, our grieving can be aggravated and prolonged.

So I ask my brothers to reflect upon the deaths in their lives. How did you grieve when these deaths entered your life? What, if anything, would you do differently today to ease your grieving the next time a death occurs?

We can also hide out or grovel in our mourning. We need to cultivate a rhythm of apartness and companionship when death occurs. I'll never forget the beautiful support of my wife and colleague, Carolyn, when she did the midnight service alone, as I drove from San Diego to Los Angeles to be with my mother upon my father's death. In twenty plus years I had only missed two ministerial duties: when our daughter was born on Father's Day morning and now on Christmas Eve when my father died. In both cases I did the right thing by choosing family over profession.

I also remember receiving a poignant poem from my spiritual kin, Kurt Kuhwald, a few days after my father's death. Such excerpts as these comforted me:

> And he, who had so much to do to bring you into light
> and time, as well as darkness, entered the darkness
> himself . . . alone, beyond time.

> How splendid that he lived so long, (saw so many stars
> turn with the dark night). How tragic that he could not
> live one year more to see you take the first steps into the
> second night of your calling . . . steps already ringing
> with the courage you have found hidden in darkness
> where the he you knew . . . now dwells.

> And we, who are your brothers, we are here, in time, and
> we stand to hold you up, against the unremitting
> emptiness of the father gone forever. The father who
> loved but could not know the heart of your choice made
> again and again to serve the aching spirits of your
> brothers and all . . . the fathers among them.

There are those of us, Tom, who do know that choice. It is known in how our hearts know you as father, brother and son.

He is gone, we are here.

There is no time, no time at all, to lose.

V. What lessons are there in the death of Moses?

One of the most grievous realizations for men is that our dreams, even if not lost, are never fulfilled. Like Moses, we don't want to die.

> Moses was 120 years old when he died, yet his eyesight was perfect and he was as strong as a young man.

Moses wasn't ready to die. Douglas Steere tells the poignant story of Philip Neri, the late-sixteenth-century founder of the Oratorian Order:

> One day a charming law student was telling of how he already had earned a degree in civil law and now was studying canon law. "What then?" Philip Neri, the listener, asked quietly. "Why then I shall be called to the bar and practice law." "What then?" murmured Philip. "Why then I shall marry and inherit a large estate from my family and raise a fine family of children." "What then?" asked Philip. "Why then I shall make a great career in the law and may even be elected an Orator of the Rota." "What then?" asked Philip once more. "Why then I suppose I shall die like everyone else." "And what then?" asked Philip, putting the penultimate question.[56]

It's not only our own death that men fear; we also resist the aging process itself. In *Necessary Losses,* Judith Viorst quotes Susan Sontag:

> "Most men experience getting older with regret, apprehension, but most women experience it even more painfully: with shame. Aging is a man's destiny, something that must happen because he is a human being. For a woman, aging is not only her destiny . . . it is also her vulnerability."[57]

I have spent an entire session on the emotional and physical signs of aging, a scary but profitable zone for men, from mid-life on, to address.

Back to Moses. Like him, modern men seldom get to our Promised Lands.

> For you shall see the land before you; but you shall not go there, into the land which I give to the people of Israel.
>
> — Deuteronomy 32:52

But if men don't get to our Promised Land during this lifetime, we can pass things onto our descendants. We can leave legacies. We can go down in history with earned acclaim like our forebrother Moses:

> And there has not arisen a prophet since in Israel like Moses, whom the Lord knew face to face, none like him for all the signs and the wonders which the Lord sent him to do in the land of Egypt, to Pharaoh and to all his servants and to all his land, and for all the mighty power and all the great and terrible deeds which Moses wrought in the sight of all Israel.
>
> — 34:10-12

Perhaps our religious family, our Israel, can reach some Promised Land. That would be our prayer as brothers: that others, like Joshua, will take up our torch, will visit and dwell in the lands of our hopes and dreams.

Nobody knows where Moses died. No human was present, yet his legacy survived him. Elie Wiesel tells of Moses' death in this poetic manner:

> You have one more minute, God warned him so as not to deprive him of his right to death. And Moses lay down. And God said: Close your eyes. And Moses closed his eyes. And God said: Fold your arms across your chest. And Moses folded his arms across his chest. Then, silently, God kissed his lips. And the soul of Moses found shelter in God's breath and was swept away into eternity.[58]

Without friends, without a memorial service, Moses dies, but not alone; God is by his side.

VI. How do you want to be remembered?

I invite brothers to answer this question with a poem, an obituary notice, a simple epitaph which fits our souls.

I chuckle when I review the epitaph sentence I composed a year ago. I was trying to cram as much as possible into one distinguished, bulging sentence:

> He was a good and gentle man, occasionally brave, often humorous, your companion in creating a loving universe.

If I live up to one-third of my envisioned epitaph, I can rest assured when my time to die comes.

VII. How are you living more meaningfully?

But most brothers are not near death, so penultimate questions are in order. In the second half of life, what ties and tasks are you pursuing and what practices and desires are you shedding?

Carl Jung rightly described the second half of life as the afternoon, the spiritual portion. This definitely is the case for men who give this question serious thought. There are material possessions to sort out and shed but most of the conversation among brothers has to do with emotional aspirations and spiritual yearnings.

VIII. What legacy will you pass on?

It is insufficient for men to speak of legacy-at-large. I find it worthwhile for brothers to talk about passing stuff on to the *men* who will follow us.

What counsel would you give the males (not just family members) taking the globe from your hands? It is heartening to hear so many brothers cheering on their heirs with phrases like "keep the faith, the focus, the fervor of Brother-Spirit alive, my compadre!"

The Quest Goes On

Our Brother-Spirit quest is never finished and certainly not exhausted by the themes covered in the preceding course.

Reverend James Curtis asks what if our real religious questions to one another went something like this:

> Why do you like a sunset?
>
> Why do you like to make money? What is money for?
>
> What was the last book you read?
>
> Do you have any friends? What is a friend anyway?
>
> Do you like your children?
>
> Do you sometimes smile or laugh in public at your
> shortcomings? Do you have any shortcomings?
>
> Has making love ever been a religious experience for you?
> If not, what went wrong?
>
> When you wake up in the morning, are you eager and
> pleased to begin another new day? If not, what's wrong?
>
> What do you long for above all else?
>
> What do you want? [59]

To keep our Brother-Spirit quest alive, then, we have to be relentless questioners, responders, then questioners again. I find it startling, yet insightful, that the tiny book of Jonah in the Old Testament closes with a question:

> And why shouldn't I feel sorry for a great city like Nineveh . . . ?
>
> — 4:11

Jonah is in the throes of a desperate self-pity fit, "It is right for me to be angry enough to die," because God is showing mercy toward Nineveh, his hated foe. So God closes the book of Jonah, on

Jonah, by stretching our horizon to be concerned about larger tribes than our own hides.

I like God's question. I like that a sacred text ends with a question rather than a preachment. But it is God's question; it might not be yours or mine.

What, my brothers, is the most burning question in your life, right now?

BALANCE

Keep your eye on the functioning of your inner being
and start from there — to read, or pray, or to do any
needed outward deeds. If, however, the outward life
interferes with the inner, then follow the inner; but if the
two can go on together, that is best of all and then we are
working with God.[1]

— Meister Eckhart

One final Biblical story (a mix of Matthew 4 and Luke 4). It is
about our elder brother, Jesus, and his coping with wilderness temptations at the start of his ministry. Note that Jesus launches his career at the age of thirty, three years from his death, so the lessons
learned on the mountain are applicable to young and old men alike.

The challenges Jesus faced and conquered are ones which brothers engage in our quest for a deeper spiritual life. The eras are different; the struggles are parallel.

You will recall that Jesus, right after being baptized by the Holy
Spirit, full of vision and power, was immediately "led up by the Spirit
into the wilderness to be tempted." The temptations which followed
were neither idle nor unattractive. They were as seductive a crop of
temptations as can be faced by earthlings. Jesus was given the chance
to be Mr. Macho, *Numero Uno* in power and prestige the world over.
The first temptation Jesus faced was to perform a miracle by changing stones into loaves of bread. The second one was to jump off the
roof of the temple, like Superman, and prove his stature as the Son

of God. The third was perhaps the most tantalizing of all. The whole world would be his, if he would only fall down and worship Satan.

The first two temptations tried to seduce our brother into wanton displays of prowess — the typical temptation which contemporary men face daily at home, play, and work. We are constantly tempted to perform to the expectations, pressures, enticements of outsiders. If we do so, we are led to believe we will be happy and successful.

The third temptation addresses our classic male hunger for absolute control. We will be in charge of the entire globe. It is ours for the taking if we simply turn over our lives to the slithery, seductive Satan.

Satan is no fool. For the final temptation he takes Jesus "to the peak of a very high mountain" and shows him the splendor and glory of his prize. Such altitude is dizzying. Mountain highs can dazzle our spirits and lure us into heady decisions.

In the background we hear the haunting question, "What does it profit us if we gain the whole world but forfeit our very souls?" The answer is "nothing at all." Jesus knew this; he chose to keep his soul. He kept his God as well. But this is no easy temptation. It hounds modern men day in and day out. May we be wise and brave enough to follow in our elder brother's footsteps and keep on our Brother-Spirit course.

Jesus turned the first temptation down because, as physically starved as he was at the time, he knew that humans don't live by bread alone. Without spiritual nourishment we perish over the long haul. Brother-Spirit comrades learn this truth too, namely, that our sacred quest for intimacy and ultimacy is life-long, not a matter of forty days and forty nights spent in retreat.

Jesus rejected the second temptation as yet another demeaning invitation for men to flaunt our shaky egos in physical prowess. Jumping off temples is symbolic of all the conquests — professional, sexual, athletic or military — which have seduced men since the beginnings of time. Today men are still tempted to show off and perform at every corner. It is only when we join Jesus in calling such feats "foolish tests" that we turn aside this temptation and stay on spiritual purpose.

Brothers learn that the fulfilling spiritual existence is an incessant quest not a series of conquests.

In all three instances, Jesus rejected *material* acquisitions or accomplishments in favor of *spiritual* allegiance and aspiration. In this encounter with Satan, Jesus is not eschewing materialism; he is only saying that we cannot worship it. He claims that the spiritual life is ultimately more rewarding and satisfying for brothers and sisters than an existence of personal power and prestige.

However, there is life after temptations. There is life after mountain retreats and wilderness trips. Men must return to the valleys to serve the vision and lessons we learned on high.

The greatest temptation of all for Jesus and us is to remain in solitude, amid nature, away from the obligations and hecticity of the valley. We men are tempted to become ascetics, to externalize our "highs," to withdraw from society and its headaches and complexities. Remaining on the mountain is tempting indeed. It always has been.

This is the perennial struggle of men attending our Brother-Spirit weekends: we don't want to go back down the hill to our homes. We are anxious that we will lose our mountaintop strength, ecstasy and radiance. As D. H. Lawrence wrote: " . . . overhead there is always the strange radiance of the mountains." We feel powerful having just met demons, Satan himself, on the mountaintop, and emerging victorious.

Yet, my brothers, we live in the valley. We are not mountain muses. Climbing the mountain and returning to the valley is the natural rhythm of the sacred quest. We need to visit the peaks, but we live on the plains of ordinariness.

In sum, the Brother-Spirit mission includes both solitariness and solidarity, time in the mountains and time in the valley, the opportunity to be both contemplative and active. As we brothers age, we can identify with what T. S. Eliot penned in his poem "Dry Salvages":

> Old men ought to be explorers
> Here and there does not matter
> We must be still and still moving
> Into another intensity
> For a further union, a deeper communion
> Through the dark cold and the empty desolation,
> The wave cry, the wind cry, the vast waters
> Of the petrel and the porpoise. In my end is my beginning.[2]

The spiritual life invites men to be examples of balance. We are called to "be still and still moving . . . " as Eliot writes. We must know when to withdraw and when to confront, when to be a resister and when to be a recluse; we must be both activist and mystic. This is our inescapable religious charge as brothers: to maintain our spiritual balance.

Jesus "returned in the power of the Spirit into Galilee." (Luke 4:14) Full of spiritual energy, transformed, our brother returned home to his work.

So do we.

ENDNOTES

Introduction

1. Henry David Thoreau, *Walden* (New York: New American Library, 1960), p. 213.

Origins

1. Walter Wink, *Transforming Bible Study* (Nashville: Abingdon Press, 1980), p. 12.

2. Perry Garfinkel, *In a Man's World: Father, Son, Brother, Friend and Other Roles Men Play* (New York: New American Library, 1985), p. 7.

3. Andrew Melton, *New Age Journal,* September/October 1986, p. 26.

4. Ibid., p. 26.

5. Samuel Osherson, *Finding Our Fathers: The Unfinished Business of Manhood* (New York: The Free Press, 1986), p. 4.

6. Elizabeth Dodson Gray, *Sacred Dimensions of Women's Experience* (Wellesley: Roundtable, 1988), p. 68.

7. Judith Viorst, *Necessary Losses* (New York: Simon and Schuster, 1986), p. 234.

8. Garfinkel, *Man's World,* p. 1.

9. Elie Wiesel, *Messengers of God: Biblical Portraits and Legends* (New York: Random House, 1976), p. 43.

10. Daniel Berrigan, *To Dwell in Peace: An Autobiography* (San Francisco: Harper & Row, 1987), p. 54.

11. Oliver Stone, *Time,* January 26, 1987, p. 56.

12. Wiesel, *Messengers,* p. 63.

13. Nikos Kazantzakis, *Report to Greco,* translated by R. A. Bien (New York: Simon and Schuster, 1965), pp. 458-59.

14. Joseph Heller, *God Knows* (New York: Alfred A. Knopf, 1984), p. 96.

15. Andrew Bard Schmookler, *Out of Weakness: Healing the Wounds that Drive Us to War* (New York: Bantam Books, 1988), pp. 40-41.

16. Wiesel, *Messengers,* p. 73.

17. Kirk Douglas, *The Ragman's Son: An Autobiography* (New York: Simon and Schuster, 1988), p. 34.

18. Wiesel, *Messengers,* p. 107.

19. Robert Moore and Douglas Gillette, *King, Warrior, Magician, Lover* (San Francisco: Harper & Row, 1990), p. 61.

20. Wiesel, *Messengers,* p. 198.

21. Robert Veninga, *A Gift of Hope: How We Survive Our Tragedies* (New York: Ballantine Books, 1985), p. 164.

22. Garfinkel, *Man's World,* p. 120.

23. James Auchmuty, *Brothers of the Bible* (Nashville: Broadman Press, 1985), p. 101.

24. Kenneth Patton, *Hello, Man* (Boston: Beacon Press, 1947), pp. 164-65.

25. Auchmuty, *Brothers,* pp. 91-2.

26. Ann James, *Christian Century,* March 1, 1989, p. 221.

Journey

1. Mark Gerzon, *A Choice of Heroes: The Changing Face of American Manhood* (Boston: Houghton Mifflin Co., 1982), p. 235.

2. George Lough and John Sanford, *What Men Are Like* (New York: Paulist Press, 1988), pp. 125-26.

3. Robert Bly, translator, *Selected Poems of Rainer Maria Rilke* (New York: Harper & Row, 1981), p. 49.

4. Rick Fields et al., *Chop Wood, Carry Water: A Guide to Finding Spiritual Fulfillment in Everyday Life* (Los Angeles: Jeremy Tarcher, Inc., 1984), p. 277.

5. Vern Curry, *Odyssey/Four: The Path of Spiritual Discipline* (Boston: Unitarian Universalist Association, 1980), p. 2.

6. Henri J. M. Nouwen, *Reaching Out: The Three Movements of the Spiritual Life* (New York: Image Books, 1986), p. 34.

7. Harry Meserve, *The Practical Meditator* (New York: Human Sciences Press, 1981), p. 117.

8. Ibid., p. 125.

9. Thomas Merton, *Parabola,* Spring 1987, pp. 26-27.

10. John J. Delaney, ed., *Saints Are Now: Eight Portraits of Modern Sanctity* (New York: Doubleday, 1981), p. 17.

11. William Houff, *Infinity in Your Hand: A Guide for the Spiritually Curious* (Spokane: Melior Publications, 1989), p. 113.

12. Franklin Abbott, ed., *Men and Intimacy* (Freedom, California: The Crossing Press, 1990), p. 10.

13. John Stoltenberg, *Refusing to Be a Man: Essays on Sex and Justice* (Portland, Oregon: Breitenbush Books, 1989), pp. 191-92.

14. Moore and Gillette, *King,* p. xvii.

15. Ibid., p. 143.

16. Charlene Spretnak, ed., *The Politics of Women's Spirituality: Essays on the Rise of Spiritual Power Within the Feminist Movement* (New York: Anchor Books, 1982), p. xx.

17. Ibid., pp. xi-xii.

18. Carol Christ, *Laughter of Aphrodite: Reflections on a Journey to the Goddess* (San Francisco: Harper & Row, 1987), p. 121.

19. David Kinsley, *The Goddesses' Mirror: Visions of the Divine from East to West* (Albany: State University of New York Press, 1989), p. x.

20. Carol Christ and Judith Plaskow, *Womanspirit Rising: A Feminist Reader in Religion* (San Francisco: Harper & Row, 1979), pp. 15-16.

21. Starhawk, *The Spiral Dance: A Rebirth of the Ancient Religion of the Great Goddess* (San Francisco: Harper & Row, 1979), p. 94.

22. Ibid., pp. 96-97.

23. John Rowan, *The Horned God: Feminism and Men as Wounding and Healing* (London: Routledge and Kegan Paul, 1987), p. 133.

24. Andrew M. Greeley, *The Merry Myth: On the Femininity of God* (New York: Seabury Press, 1977), p. 13.

25. William Willimon, *The Christian Century,* November 23, 1988, p. 1063.

26. William E. Phipps, quoted by Robert L. Schaibly in his sermon entitled "Moments of Unmeasured Love," printed in "Church of Larger Fellowship News Bulletin," November 1976, p. 4.

27. Erich Fromm, *The Art of Love* (New York: Harper & Row, 1956), p. 43.

28. Attributed to Rainer Maria Rilke, quoted in Jane Meyerding, ed., *We Are All Part of One Another: A Barbara Deming Reader* (Philadelphia: New Society Publishers, 1984), p. 231.

Circles

1. Sidney Harris, *Clearing the Ground* (Boston: Houghton Mifflin Co., 1986), pp. 157-58.

2. Alice Walker, *In Search of Our Mothers' Gardens* (New York: Harcourt, Brace and Jovanovich, Publishers, 1983), p. xi.

3. Carol Christ, *Laughter of Aphrodite,* p. 70.

4. George Lakey et al, "Off Their Backs . . . and On Our Own Two Feet" (Philadelphia: New Society Publishers, 1983), p. 14.

5. Gray, *Sacred Dimension,* p. 1.

6. Shirley Ann Ranck, "Feminist Theology: A Mandate for the Future of Liberal Religion," presentation to the Unitarian Universalist Denominational Grant's Panel, February 1985, p. 9.

7. Tom Owen-Towle, *Living the Interdependent Web: An Adult Series on Unitarian Universalist Principles* (Boston: UUA, 1987), p. 37.

8. John Beams, *Changing Men: Issues in Gender, Sex, and Politics,* Winter/Spring 1989, p. 27.

9. Owen-Towle, *Living,* p. 62.

10. Curry, *Odyssey,* p. 19.

11. Starhawk, *The Spiral Dance,* p. 102.

12. Rainer Maria Rilke, translated by M. D. Herter Norton, *Letters to a Young Poet* (New York: W.W. Norton and Co., 1962), p. 35.

13. Sam Keen, *Fire in the Belly: On Being a Man* (New York: Bantam Books, 1991), p. 132.

Themes

1. George Marshall and David Poling, *Schweitzer: A Biography* (New York: Doubleday & Co., 1971), p. 301.

2. Charles Kuralt, *On the Road With Charles Kuralt* (New York: Fawcett Gold Medal, 1985), pp. 201, 204.

3. Henri J. M. Nouwen, *Thomas Merton: Contemplative Critic* (San Francisco: Harper & Row, 1972), p. 39.

4. Nouwen, *Reaching Out,* p. 118.

5. Schmookler, *Out of Weakness,* p. 253.

6. Fyodor Dostoevsky, *The Brothers Karamazov,* translated by Andrew H. MacAndrew (New York: Bantam Books, 1970), pp. xvi-xvii.

7. Martin Pable, *A Man and His God: Contemporary Male Spirituality* (Notre Dame: Ave Maria Press, 1988), p. 35.

8. John Hayward, *Existentialism and Religious Liberalism* (Boston: Beacon Press, 1962), p. 47.

9. Joseph Heller and Speed Vogel, *No Laughing Matter* (New York: G. P. Putnam's Sons, 1986), p. 77.

10. N. K. Sanders, translator, *The Epic of Gilgamesh* (New York: Penguin Books, 1960), p. 69.

11. Garfinkel, *Man's World,* p. 73.

12. Edward Klein and Don Erickson, eds., *About Men: Reflections on the Male Experience* (New York: Pocket Books, 1987), p. 52.

13. Stuart Miller, *Men and Friendship* (San Leandro, California: Gateway Books, 1983), p. 195.

14. Irving Stone, ed., *Dear Theo* (New York: The New America Library, 1937), p. vii.

15. John Edgar Wideman, *Brothers and Keepers* (New York: Penguin Books, 1984), p. 4.

16. Dick Schaap, "My Brother, My Self," *Ms. Magazine,* September 1986, p. 64.

17. Anthony De Mello, *Taking Flight: A Book of Story Meditations* (New York: Doubleday, 1988), pp. 60-61.

18. Steve Van Matre, ed., *The Earth Speaks: An Acclimatization Journal* (Illinois: The Institute for Earth Education, 1983), p. 122.

19. Sam Keen, *Fire in the Belly: On Being a Man* (New York: Bantam Books, 1991), p. 180.

20. Pat Fleming et al., *Thinking Like a Mountain: Towards a Council of All Beings* (Philadelphia: New Society Publishers, 1988), pp. 9-10.

21. Arthur and Libby Colman, *The Father: Mythology and Changing Roles* (Wilmette, Illinois: Chiron Publication, 1981), pp. 21-22.

22. Shepherd Bliss, *Yoga Journal,* May-June 1989, p. 79

23. James Morton, "Francis: Saint of the Animals," *Creation,* September/October 1987, p. 23.

24. John A. T. Robinson, *The New Reformation* (Philadelphia: The Westminster Press, 1965), p. 115.

25. Arthur and Libby Colman, *The Father: Mythology and Changing Roles* (Wilmette, Illinois: Chiron Publications, 1988), p. 108.

26. Serena Sue Hilsinger and Lois Byrnes, eds., *Selected Poems of May Sarton* (New York: W. W. Norton, 1978), p. 74.

27. Erica Jong, *Parachutes and Kisses* (New York: New American Library, 1984), p. 328.

28. Fromm, *The Art of Loving*, p. 44.

29. Osherson, *Finding Our Fathers*, p. 178.

30. James Hillman, *Wingspan: Journal of the Male Spirit*, Winter 1990, p. 9.

31. Herbert Gold, *Fathers* (New York: Arbor House, 1962), p. 205.

32. Robert Raines, *Creative Brooding* (New York: The MacMillan Company, 1966), pp. 45-46.

33. Richard Foster, *Money, Sex and Power: The Challenge of the Disciplined Life* (San Francisco: Harper & Row, 1985), p. 91.

34. Garfinkel, *Man's World*, p. 139.

35. James Nelson, *The Intimate Connection: Male Sexuality, Masculine Spirituality* (Philadelphia: The Westminster Press, 1988), p. 33.

36. Ibid., p. 33.

37. Ibid., pp. 95-96.

38. Ibid., p. 96.

39. Raymond Smullyan, *The Tao Is Silent* (San Francisco: Harper & Row, 1977), p. 305.

40. Robert Farrar Capon, *Bed and Board: Plain Talk About Marriage* (New York: Simon and Schuster, 1965), p. 89.

41. T. S. Eliot, *The Complete Poems and Plays: 1909 - 1950* (New York: Harcourt, Brace and World, Inc., 1962), p. 96.

42. Paul Tillich, *The Shaking of the Foundations* (New York: Charles Scribner's Sons, 1948), pp. 53, 57, and 60.

43. John Haynes Holmes, *I Speak for Myself* (New York: Harper & Row, 1959), p. 286.

44. Archibald MacLeish, *New and Collected Poems: 1917 - 1976* (Boston: Houghton Mifflin Co., 1976), p. 422.

45. Clarke Wells, *Sunshine and Rain at Once* (Boston: Skinner House Press, 1981), p. 4.

46. Nikos Kazantzakis, *Zorba the Greek,* translated by Carl Wildman (New York: Ballantine Books, 1952), p. 172.

47. Rick Fields, *Chop Wood,* p. xi.

48. John Stokes, *Wingspan: Journal of the Male Spirit,* Winter 1990, p. 9.

49. Ric Masten, *Looking for Georgia O'Keeffe and Other Observations* (Carmel, California: Sunflower Ink, 1987), p. 36.

50. Douglas Steere, *Together in Solitude* (New York: Crossroad, 1982), p. 16.

51. Joseph Jastrab, "Spiritual Warrior," *In Context,* Spring 1987, pp. 48-49.

52. Michael Kaufman, ed., *Beyond Patriarchy: Essays by Men on Pleasure, Power and Change* (New York: Oxford University Press, 1987), p. 22.

53. Gerzon, *Choice of Heroes,* p. 153.

54. Danaan Perry, *In Context,* Summer 1985, p. 49.

55. Elie Wiesel, *Five Biblical Portraits* (Notre Dame: Univeristy of Notre Dame Press, 1981), p. 31.

56. Steere, *Together,* p. 96.

57. Viorst, *Necessary Losses,* p. 269.

58. Wiesel, *Messengers,* p. 204.

59. James Curtis, *Church of Larger Fellowship News,* January, 1988, p. 5.

Balance

1. Meister Eckhart, *Parabola: Myth and the Quest for Meaning,* Spring 1986, p. 3.

2. Eliot, *Complete,* p. 129.

Suggested Readings

Men

Abbott, Franklin, ed. *Men and Intimacy: Personal Accounts Exploring the Dilemmas of Modern Male Sexuality.* Freedom, California: The Crossing Press, 1990.

Abbott, Franklin, ed. *New Men, New Minds: Breaking Male Tradition.* Freedom, California: The Crossing Press, 1987.

Anderson, William. *Green Man: The Archetype of Our Oneness With the Earth.* San Francisco: HarperCollins Publishers, 1990.

Baumli, Francis, ed. *Men Freeing Men: Exploring the Myth of the Traditional Male.* Jersey City: New Atlantis Press, 1985.

Bly, Robert. *Iron John: A Book About Men.* New York: Addison-Wesley Publishing Co., Inc., 1990.

Bolen, Jean Shinoda. *Gods in Everyman: A New Psychology of Men's Lives and Loves.* San Francisco: Harper & Row, 1989.

Bucher, Glenn R., ed. *Straight/White/Male.* Philadelphia: Fortress Press, 1976.

Byers, Ken. *Man in Transition: His Role as Father, Son, Friend, and Lover.* La Mesa, California: Journeys Together, 1989.

Colman, Arthur and Libby. *The Father: Mythology and Changing Roles.* Wilmette, Illinois: Chiron Publications, 1988.

Diamond, Jed. *Inside Out: Becoming My Own Man.* San Raphael, California: Fifth Wave Press, 1983.

Druck, Ken, and Simmons, James C. *The Secrets Men Keep.* New York: Ballantine Books, 1985.

Farrell, Warren. *Why Men Are the Way They Are: The Male-Female Dynamic.* New York: McGraw-Hill Book Co., 1986.

Garfinkel, Perry. *In a Man's World: Father, Son, Brother, Friend and Other Roles Men Play.* New York: New American Library, 1985.

Gerzon, Mark. *A Choice of Heroes: The Changing Face of American Manhood.* Boston: Houghton Mifflin Co., 1982.

Gilmore, David. *Manhood in the Making: Cultural Concepts of Masculinity.* New Haven: Yale University Press, 1990.

Goldberg, Herb. *The Hazards of Being Male.* New York: New American Library, 1977.

Kaufman, Michael, ed. *Beyond Patriarchy: Essays by·Men on Pleasure, Power and Change.* New York: Oxford University Press, 1987.

Keen, Sam. *Fire in the Belly: On Being a Man.* New York: Bantam Books, 1991.

Klein, Edward, and Erickson, Don, eds. *About Men: Reflections on the Male Experience.* New York: Pocket Books, 1987.

Lough, George, and Sanford, John A. *What Men Are Like.* New York: Paulist Books, 1988.

Miller, Stuart. *Men and Friendship.* San Leandro, California: Gateway Books, 1983.

Moore, Robert and Gillette, Douglas. *King, Warrior, Magician, Lover: Rediscovering the Archetypes of the Mature Masculine.* San Francisco: Harper & Row, 1990.

Owen-Towle, Tom. *New Men — Deeper Hungers.* Carmel, California: Sunflower Ink, 1988.

Stein, Harry. *One of the Guys: The Wising Up of an American Man.* New York: Simon and Schuster, 1988.

Stoltenberg, John. *Refusing to Be a Man: Essays on Sex and Justice.* Portland, Oregon: Breitenbush Books, 1989.

Spirituality

Adler, Margot. *Drawing Down the Moon: Witches, Druids, Goddess-Worshippers and Other Pagans in America Today.* Boston: Beacon Press, 1981.

Christ, Carol, and Plaskow, Judith. *Womanspirit Rising: A Feminist Reader in Religion.* San Francisco: Harper & Row, 1979.

Daly, Mary. *Beyond God the Father: Toward a Philosophy of Women's Liberation.* Boston: Beacon Press, 1973.

Donnelly, Dody H. *Radical Love: An Approach to Sexual Spirituality.* Minneapolis: Winston Press, Inc., 1984.

Eisler, Riane. *The Chalice and the Blade: Our History, Our Future.* Cambridge: Harper & Row, 1987.

Fleming, Pat; Macy, Joanna; Naess, Arne; and Seed, John. *Thinking Like a Mountain: Towards a Council of All Beings.* Philadelphia: New Society Publishers, 1988.

Fox, Matthew. *Original Blessing: A Primer in Creation Spirituality.* Santa Fe: Bear and Co., 1983.

Gray, Elizabeth Dodson. *Sacred Dimensions of Women's Experience.* Wellesley: Roundtable Press, 1988.

Hanh, Thich Nhat. *The Miracle of Mindfulness: A Manual on Meditation.* Boston: Beacon Press, 1976.

The Holy Bible, Revised Standard Version (RSV). New York: Nelson, 1953.

Houff, William H. *Infinity in Your Hand: A Guide for the Spiritually Curious.* Spokane: Melior Publications, 1989.

Iglehart, Hallie. *Womanspirit: A Guide to Women's Wisdom.* San Francisco: Harper & Row, 1983.

Kelsey, Morton. *Companions on the Inner Way: The Art of Spiritual Guidance.* New York: Crossroad, 1983.

Kinsley, David. *The Goddesses' Mirror: Visions of the Divine from East and West.* Albany: State University of New York Press, 1989.

Nelson, James B. *The Intimate Connection: Male Sexuality, Masculine Spirituality.* Philadelphia: The Westminster Press, 1988.

Pable, Martin W. *A Man and His God: Contemporary Male Spirituality.* Notre Dame: Ave Maria Press, 1988.

Rowan, John. *The Horned God: Feminism and Men As Wounding and Healing.* London: Routledge and Kegan Paul, 1987.

Ruether, Rosemary Radford. *Sexism and God-Talk: Toward a Feminist Theology.* Boston: Beacon Press, 1983.

Spretnak, Charlene, ed. *The Politics of Women's Spirituality: Essays on the Rise of Spiritual Power Within the Feminist Movement.* New York: Anchor Books, 1982.

Starhawk. *The Spiral Dance: A Rebirth of the Ancient Religion of the Great Goddess.* San Francisco: Harper & Row, 1979.

Thurman, Howard. *Deep Is the Hunger: Meditations for Apostles of Sensitiveness.* Richmond, Indiana: Friends United Press, 1951.

Wiesel, Elie. *Messengers of God: Biblical Portraits and Legends.* New York: Random House, 1976.

MAIL ORDER INFORMATION:

For additional copies of *Brother-Spirit,* send $11.95 plus $2.00 per book for shipping and handling (add 8.25% sales tax in California). Make checks payable to the author and mail to: Tom Owen-Towle, 3303 Second Avenue, San Diego, California 92103.

Brother-Spirit is also available through local bookstores that use R.R. Bowker Company's *Books in Print* catalogue system. For bookstore discount, order through the publisher: Bald Eagle Mountain Press, P. O. Box 4314, San Diego, California 92164.